2 00

W9-BNJ-198

CRETE

THE BLUE GUIDES

BLUE GUIDE

CRETE

STUART ROSSITER

*19 Maps and Plans
drawn by* JOHN FLOWER

**ERNEST BENN LIMITED
LONDON AND TONBRIDGE**

**RAND McNALLY & COMPANY
CHICAGO, NEW YORK, SAN FRANCISCO**

FIRST EDITION 1974
SECOND EDITION 1977
THIRD EDITION 1980

Published by Ernest Benn Limited
25 New Street Square, London EC4A 3JA
& Sovereign Way : New York : San Francisco

Rand McNally & Company
Chicago : New York : San Francisco
©Ernest Benn Limited 1980

Printed in Great Britain
ISBN *Hardcover*   0 510 01620-0   528-84616-7 (USA)
ISBN *Paperback*   0 510 01624-3   528-84615-9 (USA)

PREFACE

For the many travellers who now visit Crete as an end in itself rather than as part of a tour of Greece, the BLUE GUIDE TO CRETE has amply proved its usefulness and here appears in its third edition.

The text has been considerably revised and completely reset to accord with changing conditions. Numerous new hotels have arisen; others have been enlarged; a few have changed their names. Roads have been improved and some new sections engineered, though this is of necessity a slow and continuing task in the terrain involved. Facilities of all kinds have increased with the number of tourists and in summer most of the great attractions are easier of access, either by organized excursion or through the greater number of taxis and hire cars. The standard of restaurants and the quality of food provided has risen markedly, both at the top grade and at more modest levels.

Crete has recently opened to organized tourism some of the finest beaches in Greece, notably those on the N. coast east of Rethymno, west of Khania and west of Mallia. These are backed by hotels both of first-class standards and of more modest comfort. Ayios Nikolaos and Elounda are attracting holidaymakers seeking an international class of hotel coupled with a quiet unsophisticated level of evening relaxation. Most of the resorts are now well harnessed by tour operators with charter flights from Britain, Germany and Scandinavia.

The south of the island, with cheaper and more modest accommodation, has beaches no less good if less developed from their natural state, which are enjoyed by students and long-stay travellers, many of whom arrive by land and sea by their own efforts. Here again entertainment tends to the unsophisticated. The alien discothèque has not yet become ubiquitous.

For anyone who remembers Crete even twenty years ago, the changes seem immense. Compared then with (say) Sicily, its facilities were primitive, its welcome refreshingly guileless. The visitor was welcomed to its modest and almost unadvertised resources as an interesting stranger not as the owner of a bottomless purse. To lock a car would have seemed a mortal insult. Distances seemed enormous over the badly surfaced and tortuous roads as elderly local buses toiled over mountain passes.

Speeding now along the great coastal highway, the visitor takes for granted the striding power lines, the television aerials, the radio-telephone relay stations, the large modern hotels, the growing number of taxis, the bray of the donkey giving place to the splutter of the two-stroke engine. Everywhere prosperity attendant upon an abundant food-growing economy seems apparent (the price in London of olive-oil—the main Cretan export—persuades one that it must be real). Inflation has ensured that a sum that would have kept a visitor for a week can now be spent in a day, and the island peasant still feels impelled to seek his fortune elsewhere.

It is difficult for a visitor to estimate the depth to which the very evident superficial changes may have penetrated. The innate courtesy and friendliness of Cretans still seem to be there. Of course the equable climate and the majestic mountains remain immutable. The sea, far from main shipping routes, proves notably free from pollution. It would be unreasonable to expect the manufacturers of souvenirs to offer their wares at prices lower than the undiscriminating market will stand. It is difficult to begrudge the villages a widespread distribution of electricity which brings, as well as television, the blessings of refrigeration. A marked apparent change is towards the disappearance of a male-dominated society as girls mix more freely on the beaches and in the streets. It would be presumptuous for the visitor, and it may be too soon for the inhabitant, to judge whether these changes are superficial or real and deep, and if the latter whether they are changing the soul and spirit of the island. They are in any case inevitable: even the ever-growing cost of petrol is unlikely to encourage a voluntary return to muleback.

For those without a former standard of comparison, Crete has obviously much to offer, not least a slower pace and a sunny serenity which ensures a rapid 'unwinding' from the cares of an ever faster world. The enduring features that draw the visitor to Crete are the remains of Minoan civilization, the flowers, the landscape, and the people. Though this book hardly does justice to any of these, it is hoped it will provide enough practical information and topographical guidance to lead the traveller to appreciate them for himself.

The Editor is greatly indebted to the National Tourist Organization of Greece for their generosity in sponsoring a three-week revision tour in 1979, in particular to the Director in London *Mr. Panayotis ('Peter') Analytis* and his staff, and to *Mrs. Pirounakis* in Herakleion for their faultless arrangements. Messrs *Hertz* supplied a car with a minimum of red tape, compared with which the editorial vehicle seems uncomfortable and inefficient. Gratitude is due also to *Mr. Kelvin Moyses* for much good advice over the years and to many kind correspondents who have sent informative postcards while using the book in Crete. **John Flower** has, as usual, been responsible for bringing his maps up to date.

Nobody knows better than the writer the difficulty of avoiding error, both of commission and omission, and any constructive suggestions for the improvement or correction of the guide will be welcomed.

CONTENTS

CONTENTS

MAPS AND PLANS

A BRIEF HISTORY OF CRETE

NEOLITHIC PERIOD (6000–3000 B.C.). The first inhabitants of Crete lived in caves and open settlements, as at Knossos and Phaistos. They arrived about 6000 B.C. (according to a recent radiocarbon date from Knossos), perhaps from Anatolia (Asia Minor). These first inhabitants did not use pottery (though theirs was probably not a true pre-pottery culture) but soon the characteristically Neolithic dark burnished wares came in. Stone axes and perforated maceheads and bone tools are characteristic artefacts while clay and stone female figurines, some with pronounced steatopygy, perhaps indicate the cult of a great mother goddess. Obsidian from Melos is used for small tools. Houses are simple rectangular constructions with fixed hearths.

MINOAN PERIOD (3000/2800–1100 B.C.). The Cretan Bronze Age was divided by Sir Arthur Evans into three main periods, Early, Middle, and Late Minoan (named after the legendary king Minos), and each of these has three subdivisions (I, II, III). These have been further divided in the light of new evidence. They represent supposedly inevitable cycles of growth, peak, and decline based on pottery styles and are necessarily artificial and of unequal time duration. They are therefore confusing to the layman. But, until some unquestionable fixed point of chronology can be established, they seem preferable to the more recent but vague 'pre-Palatial', 'proto-Palatial', 'neo-Palatial', based largely on 'destruction horizons' about whose causes, contemporaneity, and absolute dating there is so far no agreement.

The transition from Neolithic to Early Minoan, accompanied by an influx of new people, perhaps from Anatolia, is marked by the occupation of many new sites and by three distinct pottery styles, grey and brown wares with dark burnished patterns, and red on buff and white on red painted wares, and red monochrome wares. Gradually copper replaces stone for artefacts; by E.M. II flat leaf-shaped copper daggers are common, stone vessels and carved sealstones begin and there is very high competence in the making of jewellery. The houses, with rectangular rooms, are of more complex plan, as at Vasilike in East Crete. It is from this site that the brilliant black and orange pottery characteristic of E.M. II is best known. There is considerable variety in burial practice; already in E.M. I the circular stone-built communal ossuaries (tholos tombs) occur, especially in the Mesara, while rectangular ossuaries and chamber tombs are found in East Crete and clay coffins were used at Pyrgos on the N. coast.

In Middle Minoan I the first Palaces, witness to the presence of kings, were founded c. 1950–1900 B.C. There is fuller evidence of town life on the main sites and individual villas were built at Mallia and Khamaizi. Peak sanctuaries as on Juktas above Knossos, Petsofa above Palaikastro and at Koumasa are established. The Early Minoan tombs continue in use everywhere, but in many places a new method of burial, in clay storage jars (pithoi) is introduced. Examples of this are the cemetery at

Pakhyammos near Gournia and in the Mesara tholos tomb at Voroi. In the Palaces the M.M. I style of pottery is succeeded by brilliant thin-walled polychrome vases, M.M. II Kamares Ware. Metal techniques are more developed: daggers and swords have medial ribs, jewellery has granulation and filigree decoration, seals have elaborate patterns on the torsional principle whereby the designs find their equilibrium through revolution about a centre rather than symmetry about an axis. A hieroglyphic system of writing is invented and used on seals, clay bars, and labels. Foreign contacts are wide; Egyptian scarabs appear in Crete and M.M. II pottery in Egypt and the Near East. A few stone vessels reach the mainland and the islands. Then, c. 1700 B.C., comes a great catastrophe, probably due to earthquakes, which laid the Palaces in ruins. The same disaster doubtless overcame the town sites though it is not so easy to identify 'destruction horizons' in view of the rebuilding and adaptation of the houses.

After this great disaster the Palaces are rebuilt (in M.M. III) and the island enters on its greatest age, from soon after 1700 to c. 1450 B.C. In this period most of the Minoan buildings which survive today were constructed, notably the great villas in the country and those around the Palaces. In architecture limestone and gypsum masonry in ashlar construction is used in the Palaces and some of the villas. Open planning with courts and columned porticos was favoured; large rooms were divided by partitions and light was introduced by light wells in internal parts of buildings. Fresco paintings decorated the walls of major rooms; highly elaborate plumbing and drainage systems were installed. The extensive space devoted to magazines filled with great storage jars bears witness to the great prosperity of the age. Town sites such as Gournia, Palaikastro, and Zakro are fully developed. Foreign contacts are wide, extending to mainland Greece, where a strong artistic influence is exercised, the islands, on which several colonies are settled, Troy, Miletus, Cyprus, Rhodes, Syria, Egypt, and the Lipari Islands in the west. To these places went Late Minoan I clay and stone vessels while Crete received fine stones like Egyptian alabaster, Spartan basalt, antico rosso and obsidian for the manufacture of stone vases and sealstones. In the island a script known as Linear A is used to write an as yet undeciphered language; tablets for domestic inventories are known from Ayia Triadha, Myrtos (Pyrgos), Palaikastro, Tylissos and Zakro; inscriptions appear on large clay pithoi, on a potter's wheel and on a number of offering tables. These last are often from sacred caves or sanctuaries and their inscriptions are doubtless religious. At this time clay and stone vases, sealstones and bronzes reach their acme. Then near the end of Late Minoan IA, there is a total destruction involving all the major sites of the island. Its cause is not known for certain but it may well be the result of the great volcanic explosion c. 1470 B.C. of Thera (Santorini) to the north. Such explosions are regularly accompanied by earthquakes and this must also have caused tidal waves.

Only at Knossos was there immediate recovery and the Palace now enters on its final phase, c. 1450–1400/1380 B.C. Taking note of the presence of Linear B tablets, found only here in Crete but regularly on the mainland at Pylos, Mycenae, and Thebes, and the formalized pottery patterns known as the Palace Style, most archaeologists accept that the rulers of Knossos in this last phase were Myceneans, though from where on the mainland is not known.

CHRONOLOGICAL TABLE

BC	Egypt	Crete	Mainland		
1000—	XXI	Sub-Minoan	Proto-Geometric		
1100—	XX	LM III C			—III C
1200—	XIX	LM III B		MYCENEAN	III B
1300—	Amarna	LM III A$_1^2$	LH		III A$_1^2$
1400—	XVIII	LM II			II B
1500—		LM 1 B / LM 1 A	SHAFT GRAVES		II A / —1
1600—	Hyksos	MM III B			
1700—	XIII	MM III A / MM II B	Middle Helladic		
1800—		MM II A		PALACES	
1900—	XII	MM I B			
2000—	XI	MM I A — FAST WHEEL	(LERNA V)		
2100—	F.I.P.		FAST WHEEL EH III (LERNA IV)		
2200—	VIII–X	EM III			
2300—	VI		LERNA HOUSE OF TILES EH II (LERNA III)		
2400—		EM II C B A			
2500—	V		EH I		
2600—	IV				
2700—	III	B			
2800—	II	EM I	(LERNA II)		
2900—	I	A	Neolithic		
3000—	Pre-Dyn	Neolithic	(LERNA I)		

After M. S. F. Hood

After the great destruction some of the sites were not reoccupied, for example Mochlos, Pseira, and the large villas at Nirou Khani, Sklavokambos and Vathypetro. At other places there was reoccupation in the 14C and 13C on a reduced scale, as at Gournia, Knossos, Mallia, Palaikastro, Tylissos, and Zakro; on these sites individual houses or rooms were cleared and re-used; there was some building on a bigger scale, as at Ayia Triadha, and at least one new site, Khondros Kephala, S. of Viannos, was established. The settlement at Khania is at its most flourishing, with pottery imported from Cyprus. Shrines characterized by snake tubes and clay figures with raised arms are found, such as those at Ayia Triadha, Gortyn Mitropolis, Gournia, and Knossos. A new and distinct method of burial is introduced, with rectangular painted clay chests (larnakes), placed in chamber tombs. The pottery shows some similarities with the Mycenean wares now being spread from Italy to Syria, but in the main it goes its own independent way, no longer exercising external influences, except perhaps through Close Style, octopus-decorated stirrup vases towards the end of the Bronze Age in the 12C.

Life at this time was troubled for there was a movement of population to refuge cities on high inaccessible mountains such as Karphi above Lasithi. Knowledge about this period is still slight, but two things are noticeable: there is a continuity of cult from the Late Bronze Age to the Iron Age, as shown by the deposit of objects in sacred caves, notably the Idaian Cave on Mt Ida and the Diktaian Cave above Psykhro; and a number of Iron Age settlements have traces of Late Minoan III occupation. Gortyn, Praisos, and Vrokastro are examples. A rich cemetery at Prinias in central Crete is in continuous use from late Minoan times to the Iron Age.

GEOMETRIC AND ARCHAIC PERIODS. By the 8C Crete is a flourishing Dorian island. It is possible that Greeks speaking the Doric dialect had entered during the disturbed conditions of the early Iron Age. Homer ('Odyssey', XIX, 177) speaks of a mixed population including Dorians. The older Minoan population might have survived in the Eteocretans whose language, known from inscriptions found at Dreros and Praisos, is in a Greek script using pre-Hellenic words. Artistically the island now flourishes to a remarkable extent: it produces the decorated shields from the Idaian Cave and the hammered statuettes from Dreros; the Dedalic school with its formal statues and statuettes with wig-like hair plays a leading part in the beginnings of Greek sculpture; the Geometric pottery, especially the polychrome amphoras from Fortetsa, is distinctive; somewhat later come the Archaic relief pithoi. Fine jewellery is also produced and there are interesting clay votive relief plaques. Settlements are of all kinds, on high peaks like Vrokastro, on acropolis hills like Dreros and Prinias or on low hills like Knossos and Phaistos. Burials in tholos tombs continue from Protogeometric, if not L.M. III, into the Geometric period. Cremation is now universal.

CLASSICAL, HELLENISTIC, AND ROMAN PERIODS. From the 5C until the Roman conquest in 67 B.C., Crete is divided into many small cities, regularly on defensible hills with a saddle between two summits. Defence walls are usual, as for example at Aptera and Eleutherna. Many cities mint their own coins. There is frequent inter-city warfare. The social structure is dominated by aristocratic families. The island had Dorian institutions like those of Sparta, and the Cretan Kosmoi, like the Spartan Ephors, exercised so much control over public and private life as to draw from Aristotle the criticism that it was overdone ('Politics', II, 10). Culturally, the island offers nothing distinct from the Classical and Hellenistic world. Life cannot have been everywhere as easy or comfortable as in the Roman period when more peaceful conditions produced large spreading settlements in the low-lying or coastal areas, as with Gortyn, Knossos, or Stavromenos on the coast E. of Rethymno. Sites like Mochlos are inhabited for the first time since the Bronze Age. After the brutal conquest by Q. Metellus Creticus in 67 B.C. Gortyn became the capital of the new province of Crete and Cyrenaica and as such the residence of the governor. Villas are built, such as the Villa Dionysus at Knossos, and there is extensive public building at Aptera, Gortyn. Knossos, and Lyttos.

MEDIEVAL AND MODERN PERIODS. That Crete continued to flourish in the early Byzantine period (5-9C), is shown by the large number of basilican churches, often with mosaics and columns made from imported stones. Examples of such churches are at Gortyn (Ayios Titos), Khersonesos between Herakleion and Mallia, at Knossos, and at Vizari in the Amari valley. Then for over 100 years, c. 823–961, the Saracen Arabs conquered and held the island, though little survives from their occupation save for their coinage. The liberation was achieved by the Emperor Nikephoros Phokas, who catapulted the heads of his Mussulman prisoners into the town of Herakleion, or Kandak as it was then called. After the Fourth Crusade the Genoese ruled for the early years of the 13C until the island was sold by Boniface of Montferrat to Venice who held it for over 400 years (1210–1669). Cretan malmsey was drunk in England in the Lancastrian era and the early Tudors employed a consul to ensure its supply. Under the Venetians and after the fall of Constantinople in 1453 there was a late renaissance of Byzantine art resulting in the fresco paintings of many Cretan churches; Crete also produced many notable icon painters, Tzanfournares, Dhamaskinos, Klotzas, the famous Theotokopoulos (El Greco), who moved to Venice and Spain, and, in the 18C, Kornaros who painted the great icon in the monastery of Toplou. Three notable Cretan painters, Theophanes, Anthony, and Tzortzis, worked on the Greek mainland. In the field of literature the poetic drama, the Sacrifice of Abraham, appeared and another Kornaros produced the epic rhymed romance, Erotokritos. Khania, Rethymno, Herakleion, Ierapetra, and Siteia had their walls built or were fortified; Spinalonga, N. of Ayios Nikolaos, received a fortress to guard the natural harbour. Numerous public buildings were erected in the cities, and docks, harbours, and wharves were constructed.

The Turkish occupation (1669, the fall of Herakleion, to 1898) was exacting, and life reached the lowest level since the end of the Bronze Age. The Sublime Porte was not so much harsh as indifferent to the economic conditions of the island. Pashley in 1837 describes the poverty of life. After the insurrection of 1821 an Egyptian viceroy, Mehmet Ali, was put in charge and he had reconquered most of the island by 1840.

This whole period is punctuated by revolutions of which that of 1866 is the best known.

From 1898 to 1913 Crete was independent under a High Commissioner, Prince George, appointed by the Great Powers, Britain, France, and Russia. In 1913 the island became part of Greece and in 1922–23 took part in the interchange of populations whereby the Turkish element left and Greek refugees from Asia Minor came in, making settlements on the outskirts of the main towns. The Germans captured the island in 1941 after what is now seen as one of the decisive battles of the war. Though the allies lost it through indecisive direction by their commanders, the New Zealanders and Greeks wrote imperishable pages in their history to make it for Germany a Pyrrhic vistory. Gen. Student's 7th airborne division of 5000 élite parachutists was virtually destroyed and "never again appeared in any effective form"(Churchill). Many trapped British and New Zealand troops were aided in escaping to North Africa by Cretan partisans or stayed to join their resistance movements. During the occupation the Germans burnt a number of villages as reprisals. Since the war tourism, attracted by the climate and splendid remains of the Minoan civilization, has brought rapid prosperity to the towns which is slowly affecting also the villages.

PRACTICAL INFORMATION

I. APPROACHES TO CRETE

Crete can now be approached directly from Britain and elsewhere by charter flight; Manchester and Gatwick are the principal departure points in Britain. The approach by scheduled flight can be effected daily by changing in Athens, though the times of arrival and departure are not particularly convenient, involving late evening arrival in Herakleion and early morning departure from the island.

By sea it is possible about once a week to take ship from Venice or Ancona, disembarking at Herakleion, thus avoiding trans-shipping luggage at Piraeus. In general, however, the principal approach by sea is from Piraeus.

The approaches from Britain to the mainland of Greece are fully indicated in the 'Blue Guide to Greece'.

Travel Information and Bookings. General information may be obtained gratis from the NATIONAL TOURIST ORGANIZATION OF GREECE (in Gk. EOT), 2, Odhos Amerikis, Athens 133 (London office: 195-197 Regent St., W1). The organization does not recommend hotels, nor does it make bookings, but it issues an annual list of Tour Operators to Greece, indexed by destination and by type of holiday. There are everywhere accredited members of the Association of British Travel Agents (ABTA) who sell travel tickets, book accommodation, and market the 'package' holidays of tour operators. A wide range of holidays in Crete is offered by *Olympic Holidays Ltd,* 24-28 Queensway, London W2. Cruises including Crete in their itineraries are arranged by *Lunn-Poly Holidays,* 32 Edgware Rd, W2; 9 Glen House, Stag Place, SW1; *Swans Hellenic Cruises* (Hellenic Travellers Club), 237 Tottenham Court Rd, W1; *Fairways & Swinford (Travel) Ltd,* (Society for Hellenic Travel), 18 St George St., W1. Specialists in arranging individual Greek travel with conducted tours are *Gellatly, Hankey & Co. Ltd.,* 23 Pall Mall, SW1; and *Wings Ltd,* Wings House, Welwyn Garden City, Herts.

The following general travel agents have branches not only in many towns throughout Britain but also in Greece:

Thomas Cook & Son, 45 Berkeley St., W1 and many branches in Central London; *American Express,* 6 Haymarket, SW1, 89 Mount St., W1.

Regular Air Services between London and Athens are maintained by British Airways and Olympic Airways. From the *West London Air Terminal,* in Cromwell Road, SW7, passengers are conveyed to *London Airport* (Heathrow) by coach. Full information may be obtained from *British Airways,* 141 New Bond St., W1. Passengers from abroad to Crete avoid an awkward change of terminals in Athens by travelling Olympic Airways throughout.

Scheduled services of Olympic Airways from the Greek mainland and islands are numerous:

FROM ATHENS AIRPORT (Ellenikò) to Herakleion, 3—9 times daily
to Khania, 3—5 daily.

FROM RHODES to Herakleion, 4 or 7 times weekly.

Steamship Services. FROM PIRAEUS: Passenger and Car Ferry nightly
to *Herakleion* in 12 hrs; also nightly to Soudha (for *Khania*) in 11 hrs. To
Herakleion there are two services nightly by rival companies. Their
newest car ferries have comfortable and well-equipped cabins in both
first and second class. Tourist class accommodation in reclining seats
and improved 3rd class have replaced the former 'deck' class. At
weekends in summer there may be extra services by day. Other ships ply
weekly to *Ayios Nikolaos* and *Siteia*; from Rhodes and Karpathos to
Siteia and *Ayios Nikolaos.* An experimental service has recently been
tested in summer from Yithion and S. Peloponnesian ports to Soudha.
There are connections with Santorini and some other islands from
Herakleion, also with either Kavalla or Thessaloniki (see local
newspapers).

COMPARATIVE FARES. In July 1979 the price of fuel was rising rapidly
and fares were about to be increased in different but large percentages on
all forms of transport. It is probable that the air fare will continue to be
comparable with the first-class fare by ferry, but at what level it is
impossible to forecast.

II.   FORMALITIES AND CURRENCY

Passports are necessary for all British and American travellers
entering Greece and must bear the photograph of the holder. British
passports (£10.00) valid for ten years, are issued at the Passport Office,
Clive House, Petty France, London, SW1 (9.30-4.30, Sat. 9-30-12.30),
or may be obtained for an additional fee through any travel agent.

In general passports of the United Kingdom and Crown Colonies, of members
of the Commonwealth, of Kenya, all W. European countries, and the U.S.A. do
not require visas. Nationals of Gt. Britain and Colonies, Ireland, Australia,
Canada, New Zealand, Cyprus, or Pakistan wishing to remain in Greece must
apply after 3 months (some others including U.S.A. 2 months) for a police permit
to the nearest police station.

Health Regulations. Vaccination and inoculation are not required for entry
from Europe, Cyprus, Turkey, Canada, or the U.S.A.

Custom House. Except for travellers by air, who have to pass the
customs at the airport of arrival, luggage is examined at the frontier or at
the first Greek port of call. Normally passengers have to attend in person
at the ΤΕΛΩΝΕΙΟΝ (teloníon: custom house), but the luggage of
passengers disembarking in Crete from a foreign ship is examined on
board.

Crete is an integral part of Greece and there are no formalities
between the island and the mainland.

PRIVATE CARS may be imported for up to 4 months without customs
documents, but the formalities involve recording in the passport such
details as number of chassis, engine, etc., and the log book should be
carried. Trailers and caravans need a customs document.

Provided that dutiable articles are declared, bona-fide travellers will
find the Greek customs authorities courteous and reasonable. The
following are free from duty: books, sporting equipment, bicycle,

camera with a reasonable quantity of film, binoculars, typewriter, record-player with up to 20 records, portable radio, tape-recorder, 250 gr. of tobacco in any form, sweets (up to 10 kg. or 22lb), 2 packs of playing-cards. Sporting firearms (2 guns and 20 cartridges maximum) must be declared on entry and noted in the passport.

Souvenirs bought in Greece may be exported without licence up to a value of 4500 dr.; the souvenir shop at Athens airport is reached after weighing-in and customs. The export of olive-oil is limited to one container not exceeding 18 kg. per person. (NB: Olympic Airways require that oil is adequately sealed before allowing it on board aircraft). *The purchase of any work of art dating before 1830 is strictly prohibited, except from recognized antiquarian shops, and their export totally prohibited except with permission and a special licence.* Infringements are met with confiscation and severe penalties. This applies to potsherds and coins; licences to cover individual objects *may* be granted to scholars and institutions.

The duty-free allowance on entering the United Kingdom for travellers returning direct from a country outside the E.E.C., is (in effect) one litre-bottle spirits (*or* two litre-bottles of fortified wine or aperitifs) *and* two litre-bottles of table wine, 200 cigarettes *or* 50 cigars (or equivalent), a small bottle of perfume *and* a bottle of toilet water, and personal souvenirs to a value of £10. The E.E.C. regulations are expected to apply after 1981 when Greece becomes a ratified member. Foreign reprints of copyright English books may be confiscated.

Currency Regulations. The allowance permitted by the British Government for pleasure travel per yearly period varies from time to time. In 1979 it was a nominal £500 all of which might be held in foreign notes. In sterling notes not more than £100 may be taken out of Great Britain by British or American travellers. Not more than 1500 drachmas may be brought into or taken out of Greece in notes. There is no restriction on foreign currency, but sums over U.S. $500 (c. £300) should be declared on arrival to be entered in the passport.

Money. The monetary unit is the drachma (dr.), divided notionally into 100 lepta (l.) though in practice nothing less than 1 drachma circulates. During July 1979 the exchange value varied between 75 and 82 dr. to the pound, making the drachma equivalent to 1¼p. Bank notes for 50, 100, 500 and 1000 dr. are issued by the Bank of Greece. There are coins of 20, 10, 5, 2 and 1 dr. Particular care is necessary with all the coins since there are several types of each in circulation in a bewilderment of sizes and inscriptions and they are easily confused even by the local populace.

Banks. Banking hours, except Sun and holidays, are 8–1 and 5.30–7.30.

III.   TRANSPORT

Travelling in Greece may be divided into three stages: party travel by cruise ship and coach (well organized but not cheap), providing guided tours of selected antiquities with nights in international hotels, where the traveller is insulated from the local populace, needs no special knowledge of Greece, and will probably acquire none; individual travel by ferry and car or public transport, staying in modest hotels, which can be inexpensive and, with use of the 'Blue Guide', should produce few problems; and getting off the beaten track, taking accommodation as it is available, for which at least some previous knowledge of Crete and of Greek is advisable.

In Crete there are no railways and only a few coastal steamers.

Roads. Most main roads and the approaches to places where tourism is fostered are asphalted. Though the condition of these roads is often good, it depends on local upkeep and recent weather conditions; subsidences and potholes can be frequent, particularly through towns and villages, and the edges are often broken. Owing to the general terrain the average speed that can be safely maintained depends on gradients and curves, a fact often forgotten by dwellers in more level lands. The average journey across the island (c. 70 km.) will take c. 2 hrs. Most main roads are marked with km. stones (reading from the chief town of the nome), but everywhere realinements are modifying the distance travelled. Where road improvements are in progress, waits for bulldozing or blasting may be experienced.

A very large programme of improvement is well in hand, and conditions everywhere (except at the actual point of any roadworks) are likely to be better than indicated (allowing for seasonal hazards of landslide or snow). In general the new roads follow the older roads and tracks on courses dictated by the terrain, and their descriptions will remain valid. Round the S. coast existing sections of road will eventually be linked between Skhinias and Pirgos to form a through route.

The great highway along the N. coast, however, has been built with little respect for the terrain, and in places has been blasted on new alinements to limit gradients. Sections were opened as finished and immediately superseded an older section. In places the old road has disappeared altogether into the new. It has thus been impossible to separate descriptions of the old and the new in a completely logical manner. Although the old road follows a traditional course through villages with many twists and turns, often amid more spectacular scenery or more typical scenes, once the new, straight, easy and signposted road has been opened, it is difficult to persuade any but the most dedicated traveller to go back to the rigours of driving the old. The two have, therefore, in general been described together, and only differentiated where they are physically separated by some considerable distance. The alternatives are clearly signposted 'Old Road' and 'New Road'. The by-pass round Herakleion has yet to be finished between the Knossos road and that to Ay. Miron (c. 3 km.).

Country Buses. Services run to schedule fairly frequently between each nome capital and the chief towns of its own districts (eparchies). Few villages are not reached by bus once a day from the chief town of their eparchy; those without a formal bus service nearly always have a communal taxi (marked AGORAION) which acts in lieu of a bus. Some mountain hamlets and places on the S. coast can be reached only on foot or muleback.—Khania and Herakleion each have several routes of frequent urban buses.

Cars, jeeps, and motor cycles may be hired from agencies in the main towns and at the airports. *Hertz* provide a very good service. Petrol prices were approaching £2 per gallon in mid-1979. There are organized trips by car or coach from Herakleion, Ayios Nikolaos, and Khania to the main archaeological sites. Taxis may also be hired by the day, the itinerary and price being agreed beforehand.

Coastal Steamers. There are passenger connections between Ayios

Nikolaos and Siteia, and between Palaiokhora, Ayia Roumeli, Khora Sfakion and Ayia Galini. Passages can sometimes be arranged on coasting caiques between Herakleion, Rethymno, and Khania.

Walking. The traveller 'me ta podhiá' (on foot), especially if equipped with a tent, can go almost anywhere in safety and will probably find more local transport than he expects. Hazards not met with in England are swarming bees, fierce sheep dogs, and (least dangerous of the three) snakes. The greatest danger is probably of twisted ankles, for which reason it is advisable not to walk alone in mountainous or more remote areas. The walker will everywhere command respect, and receive the aid, of country people, who may fall in with him on the way, often with the offer of a mule ride. In this connection it is well to remember that paths used by donkeys and mules nearly always lead from one settlement to another, whereas a path made by goats is likely to peter out on a cliff edge.

IV. POSTAL AND OTHER SERVICES

Postal Information. At the main Post Offices (ΤΑΧΥΔΡΟΜΕΙΟΝ; takhidhromío) staff generally speak English or French, and notices are displayed in Greek and French. Letter-boxes (ΓΡΑΜΜΑΤΟΚΙΒΟ-ΤΙΟΝ) are painted yellow and may be marked ΕΣΩΤΕΡΙΚΟΥ (inland) and ΕΞΩΤΕΡΙΚΟΥ (abroad). Postage stamps (γραμματόσημα; gram-matosima) are obtainable at kiosks as well as at post offices. A registered letter is ἕνα τυστημένον γράμμα (éna sistiméno ghrámma).

Letters from Greece to destinations in Europe (incl. Great Britain) are carried by air, but even between Athens and London the service often takes several days. Within Greece a letter may well take longer than the visitor spends in the country, and for arranging rendezvous the telephone or telegram are indispensable.

Correspondence marked 'POSTE RESTANTE' (to be called for) may be addressed to any post office and is handed to the addressee on proof of identity (passport preferable). A fee of 1 dr. is charged. The surname of the addressee, especially the capital letter, should be clearly written, and no 'Esq.' added.

Telephones. The Greek telephone and telegraph services are maintained by a public corporation, the Ὀργανισμός Τηλεπικοινωνιῶν Ἑλλάδος (O.T.E.) separate from the postal authority. All large towns have a central office of the company, with call-boxes and arrangements for making trunk and international calls and sending telegrams. Local calls can be made from subscribers' instruments and from the many instruments available to the public at kiosks and in cafes, bars, etc. Call-box telephones are constructed to take 2 dr. pieces.

Subscriber Trunk Dialling operates to most large provincial towns and the main islands, to some countries in Europe including Great Britain (dial 0044), and to the U.S.A. (001). For other inter-urban calls dial 151 or 171 (consult directory); abroad 160 or 161; telegrams 105; police 100; time 141. Transferred-charge calls are accepted. The number of links out of Crete is inadequate to the volume of traffic and in summer there are often long delays on calls abroad.

In rural areas the service may not operate for 24 hrs per day. Connection is by radio link.

Telegrams may be sent from O.T.E. centres or main post offices. Telegrams, both inland and foreign, may be sent in English.

PARCELS are not delivered in Greece. They must be collected from the Post Office, where they are subject to handling fees, full customs charges, and often to delay. Dutiable goods sent by letter post are liable to double duty on examination. The bus companies operate an efficient parcels service between their own praktoreia (booking offices).

V. HOTELS AND RESTAURANTS

Hotels (Ξενοδοχεῖα). In Crete most, hotels of tourist category have been built, enlarged or improved in the last ten years. Much of the expansion of the last five years has been on previously deserted coasts, catering mainly for static 'package' parties of sun-seekers. The *Chamber of Commerce of Hotels of Greece* publishes an annual 'List of Hotels'; and lists are also included in the National Tourist Organization's free illustrated pamphlets covering the various regions.

There are six official categories **L** (luxury), and **A-E.** The few de Luxe hotels compare favourably with their counterparts in other countries; almost all have restaurants; their rooms all have private bathrooms and air conditioning. In all hotels of Class **A** and most of Class **B** a proportion of rooms (sometimes all) are equipped with private bath or shower. Class **C**, at present the most numerous, is the least easy to appraise. Many Greek hotels do not have restaurants. Hotels classed **D** or **E** have no public rooms and sometimes only cold water, though their standard of cleanliness and service may well be adequate for a short stay.

Cat.	Single Room		Double Room	
	without bath or shower	with bath or shower	without bath or shower	with bath or shower
L		900-1460		1200-2300
A		535-690		720-966
B	230-305	368-526	320-506	460-742
C	253	320-368	265-374	400-460
D	201	253	265	368

Hotels in Crete are nearly all of recent construction and tend to the international pattern. Except in Herakleion there are few of the traditional cheap lodging-houses found in mainland cities because local travellers generally stay with friends of friends. In the seaside villages there are everywhere modest rooms to let in private houses.

Charges are fixed annually by the Greek Hotel Association. Hoteliers may not exceed the maximum permitted figure; the charge appropriate to each room, quoted with service, porterage, and taxes included (except for Value Added Tax of 7 per cent), is entered in a notice fixed usually to the inside of the door. (Air conditioning is charged extra.) The rates actually applying in Crete at midsummer 1979 are given in the annexed table. Thus (with breakfast) a room without bath in a provincial **C** class hotel cost about £5.00, while board in a luxury hotel might well exceed £30 per day. Considerable reductions can be obtained in Nov–March.

Despite the official categorization, hotels still can vary widely. At the more popular sites it can be found that a hotel of lower category is superior in comfort and service to one flaunting an **A**, which can be pretentious in manner but indifferent in performance. The independent traveller will realize that here as elsewhere, some hotels at popular sites and at recently developed beach resorts are geared to package tours and coach groups, the result being a standard stabilized at a mediocre or take-it-or-leave-it level. Furthermore many hotels can legally insist on demi-pension terms, thus tying the visitor to the usually unimaginative set menus.

In this guide hotel charges are not quoted; instead the class is indicated in bold type. In general (but with exceptions where no alternative accommodation is available) hotels have not been included if they insist on prior reservation through agencies, a fixed period stay, or full board being taken; if they are open for short seasons only; or if they have no single rooms. The intention has been to assist the traveller to find a hotel where he has a reasonable chance of getting a comfortable room for the night and the value he has a right to expect from the class concerned. The omission of a name does not imply any adverse judgement; the inclusion equally implies no guarantee of excellence.

Tourist Police, distinguished by their shoulder flashes, will suggest alternative lodging for visitors unable to find their own accommodation. In provincial towns their help is often invaluable in finding keys to locked churches or museums.

Motels, of which there are a growing number, and seaside BUNGALOW-HOTELS partake of the same classification system as hotels.—In regions without hotels the tradition persists of lodging in private houses. Where there is no tourist police office, the traveller is best advised to seek out the local schoolmaster or postmaster.

Youth Hostels. The Greek Youth Hostel Association (4 Odhos Dragatsaniou, Athens) is affiliated to the International Youth Hostels Federation. Its hostels may be used by members of any affiliated association. Accommodation is usually simple and members are obliged to keep early hours; the overnight charge is 15–20 dr.; stay is generally limited to 5 days. There are hostels in Herakleion, Ayios Nikolaos, and Siteia.—The provision of official CAMPING SITES, though not yet widespread away from the coast, is being greatly extended.

Dining Out. In general the pseudo-international food of hotel tables d'hôte is disappointing. In restaurant and taverna, however, the standard of Greek cooking in Crete is high. The basic ingredients, largely local produce, are usually excellent so that there is a wide choice of places where Greek food can be enjoyable. The establishments listed in the text are chosen with the needs of tourists in mind; travellers making extended stays in the cities will see by their patronage which tavernas are currently accounted the best. Out of season, outside the large towns, it is not always easy to find much choice of food.

Restaurants ('Εστιατόρια). Luncheon and dinner are taken rather earlier in Crete than on the mainland of Greece and so conform more nearly to Western times. Most Estiatória display at the entrance a bill of fare, by which their price category can be gauged; they can usually provide translations into English and a waiter to interpret. Fixed-price and table d'hôte meals are found exceptionally in the restaurants of hotels catering mainly for coach parties of foreign tourists. Menus by law display for every dish a basic price and the final charge which includes all taxes and service. Where there is a wine boy (mikros), however, he receives only what is left for him on the *table* (c. 5 per cent).

The distinction between a restaurant proper and a Ταβέρνα is nowadays not clearly definable, but in general the **Taverna** is less formal, patronized for a convivial evening rather than for luncheon, and partly at least out of doors; its fare is uncompromisingly Greek. A PSITARION generally provides roasts, or charcoal-grills each order. An EXOKHIKON KENDRON (ΕΞΟΧΙΚΟΝ ΚΕΝΤΡΟΝ 'rural centre') combines the functions of café and taverna in a country or seaside setting.—The simplest kind of meal, consisting of milk, coffee, bread, butter, honey, etc., can be had in a **GALAKTOPOLEION,** or dairy. Here in provincial towns the visitor will find the nearest equivalent to breakfast obtainable. A **ZAKHAROPLASTEION,** or pâtisserie, sells pastries and confectionery, with drinks of all sorts, though larger establishments in the cities serve light meals (generally not cheap). These may be seen combined into a Galakto-zakharoplasteion.

Taverna meals are relatively cheap, a modest rural lunch costing 45–75 dr., though fish and fruit are expensive. Wine is cheaper than in England. Some extravagance is necessary even in the best restaurants to bring a bill for two up to 800 dr. (£10). The pattern of meals is less stereotyped than in England, the sharing of portions being quite usual, as is the mixing of hot and cold dishes; it is essential to order each course separately as several dishes ordered together may arrive together. In tavernas it is by no means unusual to visit the kitchen to choose one's dishes, and in waterside tavernas it is customary to choose one's fish from the ice; this will then be weighed, the price appearing on the menu per kilo. The oily content of most Greek food is too exuberant for northern tastes, and, though the local wine is a good counteragent, travellers will be well advised to keep to grills until they become used to it.

Food and Wine. The favourite Greek apéritif is *ouzo,* a strong colourless drink made from grape-stems and flavoured with aniseed; it is served with *mezédhes,* snacks consisting of anything from a slice of cheese or tomato or an olive to pieces of smoked eel or fried octopus. In Crete ouzo is often replaced by *rakí, tzikoudiá,* or *soumada,* stronger distillations without flavouring. As in Italy the Greek meal may begin with a foundation course of rice, such as *piláfi sáltsa,* or of pasta (*makarónia*), perhaps baked with minced meat (*pastítsio*), or with *tirópita* (cheese pie). Alternatives are soup or hors d'oeuvre, the latter being particularly good. *Taramosaláta* is a paste made from the roe of grey mullet and olive oil. The main course may be meat (κρέας, kreas), or fish or a dish on a vegetable base, baked (τοῦ φούρνου, too fournu), boiled (βραστό, vrastó), fried (τηγανιτό, tiganitó), roast (ψητό, psito), or grilled (σχάρας, skaras). The chef's suggestions will be found under ΠΙΑΤΑ ΤΗΣ ΗΜΕΡΑΣ (piáta tis iméras; dishes of the day). *Moussaká* consists of layers of aubergines, minced beef, and cheese, with butter and spices, baked in the oven. *Saligaria* (snails) are a speciality in parts of Crete. Many foreign dishes may appear in transliteration, e.g.: Εσκαλόπ (escalope), Σνίτσελ Χολστάϊν (Schnitzel Holstein), Μπιντόκ άλα: Ρούς (Bitok á la Russe), Κρέμ καραμελέ (creme caramelle), Σαλάτ ντέ φρουΐ (salade de fruits). Many sweets have Turkish names, and 'shish kebab' is frequently used as a synonym for *souvlakia,* pieces of meat grilled on a skewer. Also cooked in this fashion is *kokoretsi,* which consists of alternate pieces of lamb's liver, kidney, sweetbreads, and heart, wrapped in intestines. When not grilled, meat is often stewed with oil in unappetizing chunks. Greek cheeses tend to monotony; the ubiquitous *feta* is better eaten in salad or—peasant-fashion—with black pepper and oil than on its own. Sweets, however, are elaborate and varied, though more often partaken separately than as a course of a meal. Among the most popular are *baclava,* composed of layered pastry filled with honey and nuts; *kataïfi,* wheat shredded and filled with sweetened nuts; and *galaktoboureko,* pastry filled with vanilla custard.

WINE (κρασί) in Greece is generally of good quality and has greater strength than the wines of France. The vintages are becoming standardized, and some have widespread distribution. There is a large variety of unresinated table wines, white (ἄσπρο, áspro), red (μαῦρο, mávro, literally 'black'), or rosé (κόκκινο,kókkino, literally 'red'). Wine in Crete is generally excellent. At most restaurants the principal mainland varieties (e.g. Naoussa, Pella, Demestika, etc.) are available in bottle, but the local bottlings of *Minos, Gortys, Lato, Kastelli,* and *Kissamos* are just as good and cheaper. Reds are more plentiful than on the mainland (even loose in jugs) and retsina less favoured.

The MENU which follows contains a large number of the simpler dishes to be met with:

ΟΡΕΚΤΙΚΑ (orektiká), Hors d'oeuvre
Διάφορα ὀρεκτικά (dhiáfora orektiká), Hors d'oeuvre variés
Ταραμοσαλάτα (táramosaláta), see above
Ντολμάδες Γιαλανζῆ (dolmádhes Yalantzi), Stuffed vine leaves served hot with egg-lemon sauce
Ντολμαδάκια (dolmadakia), Cold stuffed vine leaves
'Ελῆὲς (ellies), Olives

ΣΟΥΠΕΣ (soupes), Soups
Σοῦπα αὐγολέμονο (soupa avgholémono), Egg and lemon soup
Σοῦπα ἀπὸ χόρτα (soupa apò hórta), Vegetable soup
Μαγερίτσα (magheritsa), Tripe soup generally with rice (Easter speciality)
Ψαρόσουπα (psarósoupa), Fish soup

ΖΥΜΑΡΙΚΑ (Zimarhika) Pasta and Rice dishes
Πιλάφι σάλτσα (piláfi sáltsa), Pilaf
Σπαγέτο σάλτσα μέ τυρί (spagéto sáltsa me tirí), Spaghetti
Μακαρόνια (makarónia), Macaroni

ΨΑΡΙΑ (psária), Fish
Στρείδια (strídhia), Oysters
Συναγρίδα (sinagrídha), Sea bream
Μπαρμπούνια (barboúnia), Red mullet
Μαρίδες (marídhes), Whitebait
'Αστακὸς (astakós), Lobster
Γαρίδες (garídes), Scampi (Dublin Bay prawns)
Καλαμαράκια (kalamarákia), Baby squids
Κταπόδι (ktapódi), Octopus
Λιθρίνια (lithrínia), Bass

ΛΑΔΕΡΑ (ladhéra), Vegetables or ΧΟΡΤΑ (khorta), Greens
Πατάτες τηγανιτὲς (patátes tiganités), Fried potatoes
Φασολάκια φρ. βουτ. (fasolakia fr. voutiro), Beans in butter
Μπιζέλια (biséllia), Peas
Ντομάτες γεμιστὲς ρῦζι (domátes yemistés rízi), Stuffed tomatoes

ΑΥΓΑ (avgá) Eggs
'Ομελέτα Ζαμπὸν (Omelétta Jambón), Ham omelette
Αὐγά Μπρουγὲ (avgá 'brouillé'), Scrambled eggs
Αὐγά ἀλά Ροὺς (avgá 'á la Russe'), Eggs with Russian salad

ΕΝΤΡΑΔΕΣ (entrádes), Entrées
Αρνάκι φασολάκια (arnaki fasolakia), Lamb with beans
Μοσχάρι (moskhari), Veal
Σηκοτάκια (sikotakia), Liver
Κοτόπουλο (kotopoulo), Chicken
Χῆνα (khina), Goose
Παπί (papí), Duck
Τζουτζουκάκια (tsoutsoukakia), Meat balls in tomato sauce
Κοτολέτες Χοιρινὲς (kotoléttes khirinés), Pork cutlets

ΣΧΑΡΑΣ (skaras), Grills
Σουβλάκια ἀπὸ φιλὲτο (souvlákia apo filéto), Shish Kebab (see above)
Μπριζόλες μοσχ. (brizóles moskh.), Veal chops
Κεφτέδες σχάρας (keftédes skháras), Grilled meat balls
Γουρουνόπουλο ψητό (gourounópoulo psitó), Roast sucking-pig
Παϊδάκια Χοιρινά (païdhákia khiriná), Pork chops

ΣΑΛΑΤΕΣ (salátes), Salads
Τομάτα σαλάτα (domáta saláta), Tomato salad
Μαοοῦλι (marouli) Lettuce
Ραδίκια (radhíkia), Chicory
Κολοκυθάκια (kolokithákia), Courgettes
Ἀγγουράκι (angouráki), Cucumber
Ἀγκινάρες (ankináres), Artichokes
Μελιτζάνες (melizánes), Aubergines (eggplants)
Πιπεριές (piperiés), Green peppers
Ρωσσικὴ (Russikí), Russian

ΤΥΡΙΑ (tiría), Cheeses
Φέτα (fetta), Soft white cheese of goat's milk
Κασέρι (kasséri), Hard yellow cheese
Γραβιέρα (graviéra), Greek gruyère
Ροκφὸρ ('Roquefort'), Blue cheeses generally

ΓΛΥΚΑ (glika), Sweets
Χαλβά (halva) ⎫
Μπακλαβά (baklava) ⎬ see above
Καταΐφι (kataifi) ⎪
Γαλακτομπούρεκκον (galaktoboureko) ⎭
Ρυζόγαλο (rizogalo), Rice pudding
Γιαοῦρτι (yiaourti), Yoghourt

ΦΡΟΥΤΑ (frouta), Fruits
Μῆλο (milo), Apple
Μπανάνα (banane), Banana
Ἀχλάδι (akhládi), Pear
Πορτοκάλι (portokályi), Orange
Κεράσια (kerásia), Cherries
Φράουλες (fráoules), Strawberries
Δαμάσκηνα (damáskina), Plums
Ροδάκινα (rodákina), Peaches
Βερύκοκα (veríkoka), Apricots
Πεπόνι (pepóni), Melon
Καρπούζι (karpouzi), Water-melon

MISCELLANEOUS
Ψωμί (psomi), Bread
Βούτυρο (voútiro), Butter
Ἀλάτι (aláti), Salt
Πιπέρι (pipéri), Pepper
Μουστάρδα (moustárda), Mustard
Λάδι (ládhi), Oil
Ξεΐδι (Xídhi), Vinegar
Γάλα (ghála), Milk
Ζάχαρι (zákhari), Sugar
Νερό (neró), Water
Παγωμένο (pagoméno), Iced
Παγωτό (paghotó), Ice cream
Λεμόνι (lemóni), Lemon

In Crete availability of vegetables and fruit tends even more than on the mainland to be strictly seasonal but there are several crops of tomatoes, etc.

The traditional Greek Cafe (ΚΑΦΕΝΕΙΟΝ) of the villages is an austere establishment usually thronged with male patrons for whom it is both a local club and political forum. Casual customers generally occupy tables outside. Coffee (καφέ) is always served in the 'Turkish' fashion with the grounds, Unless otherwise ordered it is heavily sweetened (*variglikó*). To obtain a less sweetened cup one orders *kafé métrio*, or if desired without sugar *skéto*. Cafes displaying the sign ΚΑΦΕΝΕΙ-ΟΝ-ΜΠΑΡ (Cafe-Bar) also serve drinks.

VI.   GENERAL HINTS

Season. Crete is generally dry and warm without extremes at sea level, except that the S. coast may be uncomfortably hot in summer. The sea is warm enough for swimming in April-November (or December on the S. coast). Amounts of rain or snow (mostly in Dec to March) vary widely throughout the island, being heavy in certain mountainous areas. In these months travel across the mountains may be subject to snow. The prevailing N. wind can be strong and cool even in summer.

Antiquities. The antiquary goes to Crete for Bronze Age sites. The Classical and Roman sites are of interest almost entirely for their commanding or attractive positions. Nowhere in Crete are there Greek buildings comparable with those in Sicily or Roman remains on the Anatolian scale. Byzantine relics are on a small scale, and Venice has left imposing signs of her power rather than fine examples of her architecture.

Use of Time. Both the serious student who needs constant access to the Archaeological Museum, and anyone seeking an easily attainable single centre from which to radiate, have perforce to choose Herakleion. The holidaymaker who wishes to combine a number of excursions with a comfortable stay on the coast is better advised, once he has seen Knossos and the Herakleion museums, to choose either Ayios Nikolaos or Khania, or divide his time between them. Daily excursions can then be made by bus, coach, or more comfortably by taxi, to the E. and W. parts of the island respectively. If he can command a car, a base can be made at one of several excellent beach hotels.

The determined touring motorist can see the greater part of the island in three weeks, the most immediately appealing aspects in less. By following the routes of this book selectively, he should be able to adapt the information to his particular interests. To explore the byways is possible only on foot or on mule or donkey-back, where time and hard living are not considered and the rewards incommensurate.

For those limited to a week, the following suggestions may be helpful. The Archaeological Museum at Herakleion (Rte 1) and Knossos (Rte 2) are a duty and pleasure that can hardly be gainsaid. The excursion to Phaistos and Ayia Triadha (Rte 4) can be combined with a bathe and picnic at Mátala. Mallia (Rte 5) can be visited on the way to Ayios Nikolaos, from which the beauties of the Gulf of Mirabello (Rte 8) can be enjoyed while visiting Gourniá, Kritsá, and Lato (Rte 7). Arkadi (Rte 13) can be briefly seen on the way to Khaniá (Rte 14), while Aptera and Akrotiri both afford fine views of Soudha Bay at the cost of a small diversion, and Rethymno can be visited on the return.

Those venturing farther afield in search of fine scenery should include Omalo and the Samaria Gorge, the Lasithi Plain and Mt Diktys, the S. coast round Frangokastello, the W. coast round Falasarna, the Rodopos peninsula, Ierapetra, Siteia and the E. coast between Vai and Zakro.

Returning travellers wishing to explore Crete beyond the tourist rounds have still the Amari plain, the Asterousia Mts., and much of the S. coast to seek out. Beyond where the asphalt ends those who are prepared to live as the Cretans live can still discover the joys and the hardships of the simple life; though in the last few years power lines and improved stone roads have brought even television to the depopulated remoter areas.

Museums and Archaeological Sites. In places most visited by tourists the way to ancient remains is generally signposted and the sites enclosed, an admission charge being levied varying between 15 and 50 drachmas. On Sun admission is free. The opening hours of museums and archaeological sites vary according to season, and, in certain cases, even to region. Generally, however, there are two set periods: 'summer' runs from 16 March to 14 October, and 'winter' from 15 October to 15 March. The NORMAL HOURS of opening are:
MUSEUMS

Summer 8-1, 3-6 Sun & hol from 10

Winter 10-4.30, Sun & hol 10.30-2.30

ARCHAEOLOGICAL SITES

Summer 8-sunset, Sun & hol 9-3

Winter 9-sunset, Sun & hol 10.30-2.30

Both museums and archaeological sites remain closed on 1 Jan, 25 Mar, Good Friday morning, Easter Holiday, and Christmas Day.

In general photography (hand cameras only) is free on archaeological sites, and may be indulged freely (save where unpublished material is on display) in museums on purchase of a second ticket for the camera. ΑΠΑΓΟΡΕΥΕΤΑΙ (apagorévetai) means forbidden. Standard fees (not cheap) are chargeable for using tripods, etc.

The Greek Antiquities Service treats its visitors' safety as their own responsibility. Travellers should, perhaps, be warned that holes are not generally fenced, nor heights guarded by railings; the very nature of archaeological remains ensures the maximum number of objects that can be tripped over. It is particularly dangerous to move about while reading or sighting a camera.

Assistance beyond that given in the text can usually be canvassed from the locals with the use of the following vocabulary: *yia* (towards) *ta arkhaia* ('ancient things), *to kastro* (any fortified height), *tis anaskafés* (excavations), *to froúrio* (medieval castle). Country peasants rarely have any idea of periods of chronology, whereas intelligent schoolboys sometimes have a surprising knowledge of the local antiquities. To locate remains on outskirts of larger villages, it is sometimes helpful to inquire at the post office.

Orthodox churches (usually open) may be visited at any reasonable hour; when they are closed a boy should be sent to look for the key (kleidhí). Women are not permitted to enter the sanctuary.

Expenses. Two levels of prices apply in Crete. Whereas simple food and accommodation in rural areas (particularly in the south) are still cheap by European standards, charges for holiday accommodation and luxury goods in the tourist resorts are scarcely lower than anywhere else in the Mediterranean.

Health. Heat and food alike may cause gastric disorders in all but the strongest stomachs; plain unsweetened lemon-juice with soda-water can be efficaceous. Chemists' advice is generally knowledgeable. When driving the midriff should be protected (a thick bathing towel is useful) from the direct rays of the sun through glass. Dishes involving reheating and made-up dishes are best avoided, especially in the evening. The Greeks are great water-drinkers and the water need not be feared in Crete. Those intending to camp other than at recognized sites may consider inoculation against tetanus. Dog bites need immediate treatment.

Public Holidays. Official public holidays in Greece are: New Year's Day; 6 Jan (Epiphany); Kathara Deftera ('Clean Monday'), the Orthodox shrove Day; 25 March (Annunciation; Independence Day); Orthodox Good Friday, Easter and Easter Monday, Ascension Day; 15 Aug (Assumption); 28 Oct 'Okhi' day (see below); Christmas Day; and 26 Dec (St Stephen). In addition to the normal religious and national festivals of Greece (comp. below), in Khania there are festivities in late-May (Anniv. of Battle of Crete); in Sfakia on 26 May and in Ierapetra on 3 Oct (both for Anniv. of 1821 Revolution); and in Herakleion on 11 Nov, the feast of her patron saint (Ay. Minas).

Carnival after three weeks' festivities reaches its peak on the Sunday before Clean Monday with procession and student revels. Procession of shrouded bier on *Good Friday;* 'Christos anesti' (Christ is risen) celebration, with ceremonial lighting of the Paschal Candle and release of the doves, in front of churches at midnight preceding *Easter Sunday,* followed by candlelight processions and 'open house'. Roasting of Paschal lambs and cracking of Easter eggs on morning of Easter Day.—*Okhi Day,* commemorating the Greek 'no' (ὄxz) to the Italian ultimatum of 1940, is celebrated with remembrance services and military processions.

Shops are open on weekdays from 8 to 1 p.m. (till 1.45 p.m. in May-Oct) and from 4–7.30 (5–8 in May-Oct). On Wed and Sat in summer they open 8–2 p.m. only; on Sat in winter, from 8.30–2 p.m. In large towns chemists take turns to offer a 24 hr service; duty chemists in Herakleion are listed in 'The Week in Herakleion', or may be discovered by dialling 173 on the telephone. Characteristic products of genuine rural industries may be sought in monasteries, local bazaars, and markets, and in village homes, the best value being in carpets, embroidery, leather-work, and pottery.

The PERIPTERO (Περίπτερον), or kiosk, developed from a French model, is a characteristic feature of Greek urban life. Selling newspapers, reading matter, postcards, cigarettes, chocolate, toilet articles, roll film, postage stamps, etc., kiosks are open for about 18 hrs a day.

Language. A knowledge of ancient Greek is a useful basis, but no substitute, for the study of modern Greek. Apart from the unfamiliarity of modern pronunciation many of the commonest words (e.g. water, wine, fish) no longer come from the same roots. Fluency in modern Greek will add greatly to the traveller's profit and experience, but those who know no language but English can get along quite comfortably anywhere on the main tourist routes. A knowledge of at least the Greek alphabet is highly desirable, however, since street names, bus destination plates, etc., cannot otherwise be read. A smattering of Greek will often result in the traveller answering more questions than he asks, though it will certainly ensure greater contact with the local populace.

The Greek alphabet now as in later classical times comprises 24 letters:

Α α, Β β, Γ γ, Δ δ, Ε ε, Ζ ζ, Η η, Θ θ, Ι ι, Κ κ, Λ λ, Μ μ, Ν ν, Ξ ξ,
Ο ο, Π π, Ρ ρ, Σ σ ς, Τ τ, Υ υ, Φ φ, Χ χ, Ψ ψ, Ω ω.

VOWELS. There are five basic vowel sounds in Greek to which even combinations written as diphthongs conform: α is pronounced very short, ε and αι as e in egg (when accented more open, as in the first e in there); η, ι, υ, ει, οι, υι have the sound of ea in eat; ο, ω as the o in dot; ου as English oo in pool. The combinations αυ and ευ are pronounced av and ev when followed by loud consonants (af and ef before mute consonants).

CONSONANTS are pronounced roughly as their English equivalents with the following exceptions; β = v; γ is hard and guttural, before a and o like the English g in hag, before other vowels approaching the y in your; γγ and γκ are usually equivalent to ng; δ = th as in this; θ as th in think; before an i sound λ resembles the lli sound in million; ξ has its full value always, as in ex-king; ρ is always rolled; σ (ς) is always hard, never like z; τ is pronounced half way between t and d; φ = ph or f; χ, akin to the Scottish ch, a guttural h; ψ = ps as in lips. The English sound b is represented in Greek by the double consonant μπ, d by ντ. All Greek words of two syllables or more have one accent which serves to show the stressed syllable. The classical breathing marks are still written but have no significance in speech. In the termination ον, the n sound tends to disappear in speech and the ν is often omitted in writing.

TRANSLITERATION has been done in this volume to the rules used in the 'Blue Guide to Greece' in order not to cause confusion. It is, however, somewhat less satisfactory as a guide to local pronunciation, which is considerably softer in Crete than on the mainland. In Ἅγιος, for example, the 'γ' is nearer to 'j' than to either our 'y' or the signposts' 'gh'; and in Crete both κ and χ approach the 'ch' of church, or even 'sh', rather than the 'ch' in loch.

Manners and Customs. CALENDAR AND TIME: Greece abandoned the Julian calendar only in 1923 so that even 20C dates can be in Old or New Style. All movable festivals are governed by the fixing of Easter according to the Orthodox calendar. Greece uses Eastern European Time (2 hrs ahead of G.M.T.); π.μ.—a.m. and μ.μ.—p.m. When making an appointment it is advisable to confirm that it is an 'English rendez-vous', i.e. one to be kept at the hour stated. The siesta hours after lunch (often late) should not be disturbed by calling or telephoning; an invitation to tea implies the arrival of the guest c. 5.30–6 p.m.

Attention should be paid by travellers to the more formal conventions of Greeks. The handshake at meeting and parting is de rigueur, and inquiry after the health taken seriously. The correct reply to καλῶς ὡρίσατε (kalós orísate: welcome) is καλῶς σάς βρήκαμε (kalós sas vríkame: glad to see you). To the inquiry τί κάνετε; (ti kánete; how do you do?) or πῶς εῖσθε; (pos íste; how are you?) the reply should be καλά, εὐχαριστῶ, καὶ σεῖς (kalà ef kharistó, ke sis): well, thank you—or ἔτσι καί ἔτσι (etsi ke etsi), so-so—*and you?* General greetings are χαίρετε (khérete; greetings, hallo) and Στό καλό (sto kaló; keep well), both useful for greeting strangers on the road. Περαστικά (perastiká) is a useful word of comfort in time of sickness or misfortune meaning 'may things improve'. It is still customary to greet shopkeepers, the company in cafés, etc., with καλημέρα (kalyiméra: good day) or καλησπέρα (kalyispéra: good evening). Σᾶς παρακαλῶ (sas parakaló: please) is used when asking for a favour or for information, but not when ordering something which is to be paid for, when Θά ήθελα (tha íthela; I should like) is more appropriate. The Greek for yes is ναί (né) or, more formally, μάλιστα (málista); for no, όχι (ókhi).

In direct contrast to English custom, personal questions (showing interest in a stranger's life), politics, and money are the basis of conversation in Greece, and travellers must not be offended at being asked in the most direct way about their movements, family, occupation, salary, and politics, though they will usually find discussion of the last singularly inconclusive.

By Greek custom the bill for an evening out is invariably paid by the host; the common foreign habit of sharing out payment round the table is looked upon as mean and unconvivial, and visitors valuing their 'face' will do it discreetly elsewhere. A stranger is rarely allowed to play host to a native and may find, if he tries, that the bill has been settled over his head by his Greek 'guest'.

It is not good manners to fill a wine-glass, nor to drain a glass of wine poured for one, the custom being to pour it half full and keep it 'topped up'. If you drain it, you implicitly suggest you are ready for more. Glasses are often touched with the toast εἰς ὑγείαν σας, your health (generally shortened in speech to the familiar yásas or yámas, or, to a single individual, yásou); they are then raised to the light, the bouquet savoured, and the wine sipped before drinking (thus all five senses have been employed in the pleasure).

Entering a Greek house one may formally be offered preserves with coffee and water; this must never be refused. Strictly to conform to custom the water should be drunk first, the preserves eaten and the spoon placed in the glass, and the coffee drunk at leisure. Payment must, of course, never be offered for any service of hospitality. Often the only way of reducing an obligation is by making a present to a child of the house. Cigarettes are often useful where a money gratuity is out of place. Equally hospitality should not be abused; those offering it nearly always have less resources than their foreign guests—even the proverbially poor student.

The 'Volta', or evening parade, is universal throughout provincial Greece. Fasting is taken seriously in Lent.

Equipment. The light in Greece is strong, even in winter, and sun glasses will be needed. Crete is dusty: a clothes brush is essential. Binoculars greatly enhance the pleasure of travel among mountains or islands. An electric torch is useful, especially in the country. A duffel-coat and a rug are great assets if intending to travel 'deck' on Greek boats.

Newspapers. Foreign-language newspapers are readily obtainable in the main towns but (because flown in) exceedingly expensive.

Weights and Measures. The French metric system of weights and measures, adopted in Greece in 1958, is used with the terms substantially unaltered. Thus μέτρο, χιλιόμετρον (khiliómetro), etc. Some liquids are measured by weight (κιλό, etc.), not in litres. The standard unit of land measurement, the *stremma*, is equal to $\frac{1}{4}$ acre. Although its use is now illegal, the old Greco-Turkish standard of weight, the *oka*, divided into 400 *drams*, may still be encountered in country districts. An oka is just under 3 lb.; 35 drams may be taken as a ¼ lb.; 140 dr. as 1 lb.

EXPLANATIONS

TYPE. The main routes are described in large type. Smaller type is used for branch-routes and excursions, for historical and preliminary paragraphs, and (generally speaking) for descriptions of minor importance.

ASTERISKS indicate points of special interest or excellence.

DISTANCES are given cumulatively from the starting-point of the route or sub-route in miles and kilometres. Road distances have been calculated where possible from the km. posts on the roads themselves, otherwise from measurement on official maps; constant realinements make it certain that these distances will vary slightly from those measured by motorists on their milometers. Shorter (walking) distances especially have been given in miles rather than kilometres, in the belief that (whatever the reformers may have in store) this accords with the instinctive preferences of both English and American readers. A Greek asked a walking distance will always give the answer as a walking *time*. Archaeologists, however, invariably use metres and the site plans are accordingly scaled in metres.

HEIGHTS are given in the text in English feet, on the maps in metres.

POPULATIONS are given in round figures according to the Census of 1971.

ABBREVIATIONS. In addition to generally accepted and self-explanatory abbreviations, the following occur in the Guide:

A´, B´	tou Protou (i.e. 'the first'), the second, etc.	km.	kilometre(s)
		J.H.S.	Journal of Hellenic Studies
Akr.	Akroterion (i.e. Cape)		
Ay.	Ayios, Ayia, etc. (Saint or Saints)	l.	lepta; left
		Leof.	Leoforos (Avenue)
B.C.H.	Bulletin de Correspondance Hellenique	m.	mile(s)
		NR	no restaurant
B.S.A.	Annual of the British School at Athens	N.T.O.	(see below)
		Od.	Odhos (Street)
c.	circa	Plat.	Plateia (Square)
C	century	r.	right
DPO	(at least) demi-pension obligatory	R.	rooms
		Rest.	restaurant
dr.	drachma(s)	Rte	route
fl.	floruit		

E.O.T. (N.T.O.)	Ἑλληνικός Ὀργανισμὸς Τουρίσμου (National Tourist Organization).
K.T.E.Λ. (K.T.E.L.)	Κοινόν Ταμείον Εἰσπράξεων Λεωφορείων (Joint Pool of Bus Owners); on plans = Bus Station.
O.T.E.	Ὀργανισμὸς Τηλεπικοινωνιῶν Ἑλλάδος (Greek Telecommunications Organization); on plans = Telegraph Office.

CRETE

Among the islands of the Mediterranean **CRETE**, in Greek *Kríti*
(KPHTH), because of its position and size has always been of para-
mount importance. Lying across the southern Aegean basin, it forms a
link in the chain through Kythera to the mainland of Greece, through
Kasos and Karpathos to Rhodes and Turkey, while to the S. the coast of
Africa is but 200 m. away. The island, 160 m. long and 36 m. wide, is
dominated by its great mountain backbone: in the W. the White
Mountains (Lefka Ori, 8045 ft), the massif of Mt Ida (Psilorites, 8060 ft)
in the centre, to the E. of which are the Lasithi Mountains (Spathi, 7045
ft), and at the eastern end the Thripte range (4840 ft) guarding the
narrow isthmus of Ierapetra. These mountains are mainly limestones of
all periods from Tertiary to Carboniferous set on a schist, phyllite or
crystalline bed. The schists have obtruded in many places at the western
end and there is much dolomite in the E.; other areas are considerably
metamorphosed, out-crops of serpentines, chlorites, talc, and gypsum
occurring in the foot-hills of the main ranges. These slope gently to the
N. and very sharply on the southern coast. This has meant that
habitation is concentrated on the N. coast around and behind the great
bays of Kastelli, Khania, Soudha, Rethymno, Herakleion, and Mirabello. By contrast the southern coast cannot support much of a population
and there is only one town, Ierapetra. The large and fertile Mesara plain,
watered by the Ieropotamos stream, is the only cultivable area of any
size in the south. An interesting geographical feature is the incidence of
high upland plains enclosed by a ring of mountains. Such are the Lasithi
plain, that of Nidha on Mt Ida and the Omalo in the White Mountains.

Lying along and just above the 35th parallel of latitude, the island is
farther S. than Algiers or Tunis. The favourable climate enables olives,
grapes, carobs (Crete produces most of the world's crop), bananas,
melons, peaches, and numerous other fruits to be grown in the lower
regions and potatoes, onions, and apples on the higher plains. Cretan
oranges are said locally (with some justification) to be the best in the
world. Tomatoes, with some forcing, are produced all the year round.
The climate and position are responsible for the island's astonishing
variety of wild plants and flowers. There are many hundreds of known
species including over 130 peculiar to Crete. In particular many varieties
of orchid and ophrys are to be found in the spring. The only wild animals
now found are the Cretan ibex (kri-kri), badger, wild cat, and weasel.
The bird life is very varied, ranging from tiny species to the heron and
golden eagle. Reptiles are less widespread than on the mainland, though
the viper is known. Scorpions are not uncommon and there is a
dangerous species of poisonous spider, the rogalidha, though as it lives
in underground burrows this is rarely seen.

There is very little industry, apart from a few small factories in or near
the main towns and a number of gypsum quarries and limestone

workings for cement. The greatest concentration of the total population (456,000 inhab.) is in the centre of the island. Above a quarter lives and works in the main towns, Herakleion, Khania, and Rethymno, the remainder in the villages, where most of the work is concerned with the vines and olives, though local weaving and tanning are done. In some areas, espescially in the S., rural depopulation is distressingly notice-able. Even the olive harvest can be brought in only with the help of foreign labour.

Crete is, however, now very conscious of the tourist potential of scenery and archaeology, and once remote areas are already being equipped to receive crowds of visitors. Road-building is everywhere in progress, including an E.-W. highway to serve the S. coast. On the N. coast large holiday hotels are increasing in number along many stretches, and it is official policy to open up the S. coast.

To the intelligent visitor the material remains of the island's history will always be the chief objects of interest, especially the Minoan palaces, towns, and villas, the Classical and Roman cities of Gortyn, Lato, and Aptera, and the products of these former civilizations, chiefly in the Archaeological Museum of Herakleion. Nor should the evidences of more recent history be neglected, notably the large number of churches with fresco paintings (Crete was the home of a brilliant late Byzantine school) and Venetian buildings in the large towns. But the direct and always generously offered friendship of the Cretan people also enables anyone who will to enjoy the modern life of the island, especially at the local church festivals (panayiri).

I. HERAKLEION AND EASTERN CRETE

1 HERAKLEION

HERAKLEION, or Iráklion (ΗΡΑΚΛΕΙΟΝ), known also by its medieval name of *Candia*, lies midway along the N. coast of Crete, of which it is the most considerable city. By population (77,500 inhab.) it ranks fifth among the cities of Greece (after Athens, Salonika, Piraeus, and Patras). Enjoying a central position, good communications with the mainland, and a high standard of accommodation, it provides the obvious centre for a first exploration of the island; and, though the town itself consists largely of formless concrete-framed buildings, the medieval street plan endures, together with much of the enceinte; in any event the splendid contents of its museum and the proximity of Knossos make it for the visitor one of the most important objectives in the Aegean.

Airport, just E. of the city; services, see p. 15.

Hotels. With restaurant, but DPO: **Astoria** (Pl. b), 145 R.; **Atlantis** (Pl. e), 135 R.; **Xenia** (Pl. f), all with swimming pool; **Astir** (Pl. a), these **A. Mediterranean** (Pl. k) **B.**

Without restaurant and less expensive: **Castro** (Pl. i), **Esperia** (Pl. j), **Cosmopolite** (Pl. c), all **B; Daedalus** (Pl. p), **El Greco** (Pl. m), **Olympic** (Pl. o), **Park** (Pl. h), **Selena** (Pl. g), **Domenico** (Pl. l). **Herakleion** (Pl. n). **Knossos** (Pl. d). all **C.**

Outside the city: **Galini, Poseidon, Pasiphae,** in suburban Poros, to the E., **C. Youth Hostel** (120 beds), 24 Khandakos.

Restaurants and Tavernas (the distinction is blurred and a leisurely relaxed atmosphere not easy to find): *Maxim*, next to Park Hotel, good; in the street of tavernas linking Od. Evans and Od. 1866; also *Minos, Klimataria*, in Od. Daidalou; *Caprice, Knossos*, opp. Morosini fountain; *Psaria*, at foot of Od. 25 Avgoustou; and others on quay W. of the harbour; also at the hotels.—Good CAFÉS in Elevtherias Sq. and ZAKHAROPLASTEIA in Vas. Konstandinou.

Post Office, Plat. Daskaloyiannis.—O.T.E. CENTRE; OLYMPIC AIRWAYS OFFICE, SHIPPING OFFICES, BANKS, etc. in Od. 25 Avgoustou.—N.T.O.G. REGIONAL INFORMATION BUREAU, 1 Od. Xanthithidou, near the Arch. Museum.

Buses through the town and to *Knossos* (No. 2) from the Harbour. To *Rethymno* and *Khania* from Historical Museum; to *Ayios Nikólaos, Ierapetra,*

33

and *Siteia;* and to *Mallia,* from Bus Station on quay below Leoforos Beaufort (see plan); to *Phaistos* from Pantokrator Gate.

Cruise Boats moor by the Port Offices, opposite the Bus Station; regular **Ferries** by the Passenger Terminal farther E.

Coach Excursions to all parts of the island; by Creta Tours, who publish 'This Week in Crete' (free), Zeus Tours, and others.

History. In the prehistoric period there was a Minoan harbour town and cemetery in the Poros suburb on the E. side of the modern city. On the heights to the S. of this, above the Kairatos stream bed, a Neolithic settlement existed. Much later in Roman times, *Heracleium* was the harbour of Knossos (Strabo, x, 476, 7). After the Saracen conquest c. 823-28 the town was named *Kandak* from the great ditch dug round it. It became the centre of piracy and the principal slave market of the Mediterranean. Nikephoros Phokas liberated it in 961 and during the second Byzantine period (961–1205) its name was corrupted to *Khandax* (the city of this period extended to the existing Khandakos and Daidalou streets). When Crete passed to the Venetians in 1210 they made the city their capital, calling it and the the island *Candia*. The impressive walls, gates, bastions, and fortifications were built over a long period (14–17C) to make Candia one of the leading seaports of the East Mediterranean. In 1538 the military engineer Michele Sammicheli came to take charge of their construction and here, in 1570, Fr. Laparelli da Cortona (the architect of Valletta) died of plague. Venice appointed a governor, known as the Duke of Crete. To develop the city it was enacted that the Venetian nobility and Greek aristocracy must build houses in it and reside there for part of the year.

Discontent with Venetian rule brought a series of revolts from within the island but in 1648 an external oppressor, the Turk, began the great siege of the city. This was to last more than 21 years. The Turkish camp lay on the hill of Fortetsa, c. 3 m. S., whence their cannons operated against the town. In the siege it is said that the Venetians and their allies lost 30,000 men, the Turks 118,000. Relief forces were sent out by Louis XIV in 1668 and 1669 under the Dukes of Beaufort and of Navailles. A sortie involved the destruction of Beaufort and his force and the remaining French withdrew. On 5 Sept 1669 the Venetian commander, Francesco Morosini, surrendered and the Venetians were allowed to leave Crete unharmed. Under the Turks the town, known now as *Megalo Kastro*, was the seat of a Pashalik. It was renamed *Herakleion* after Turkish rule ended in 1898. Though Khania was then made the capital, Herakleion, because of its central position, grew rapidly to become the chief commercial city.

A   THE TOWN   ·

In the centre of the town is Plateia Venizelou with the **Morosini Fountain**, constructed in 1626–28 by the Venetian Governor, Francesco Morosini the elder. The lions are older (14C); below the basins are reliefs with marine scenes. Opposite the fountain is *St Mark's Hall*, formerly the Venetian church of St Mark, restored since 1956 and used for lectures and concerts. It was rebuilt after an earthquake in 1303 and repaired after another in 1508; in Turkish times it was converted into the Defterdar Mosque, and the base of the minaret may still be seen to one side of it. The hall now houses a permanent exhibition of copies of fresco paintings from Cretan churches (adm. 3 dr.).

From the fountain ODHOS IKOSIPENDE AVGOUSTOU (25 Aug), since Venetian times the principal commercial street and today lined with banks and travel and shipping agents, runs down to the harbour. On the right is the newly constructed but not quite finished copy of the 16C Venetian *Loggia*; the original, much decayed, succumbed in the Second World War. This backs on to the Venetian Armoury, now used as the *Dhimarkhion*. On the N. side of this building is a relief from the *Sagredo Fountain*, also Venetian. Just beyond the loggia, in a shaded square,

stands the church of *Ayios Titos*. The original Byzantine church under-
went many reconstructions before its destruction by earthquake in 1856.
The present building was built as a mosque in 1872. A reliquary with the
head of St Titus, which the Venetians took with them in 1669, was
returned from St Mark's in 1966.

The small inner *Harbour* is guarded by the ROCCA AL MARE, a
Venetian fortress of 1523–40 (adm. 5 dr.; 9–1, 4–7; closed at 1 on Sun &
hol.), still better known by its Turkish name of *Koules*. Recently
restored, it comprises 26 chambers, including the apartments of the
garrison and stores of cannonballs. On three side are fine sculptured
Lions of St Mark (defaced; best to seaward). The battlements afford a
good view of the shipping.

Leoforos Koundouriotou fronts the old harbour, where the remnants
of several Venetian buildings are being imaginatively reconstructed.
Beyond the harbour area, to the W. are the gaunt walls of the Venetian
cathedral of St. Peter. The well-preserved vaulted *Arsenals*, also 16C, on
the quay opposite the Port Offices of the modern harbour, are now used
as warehouses. Eastward extend the modern passenger quays.

From just W. of the Bus Station, the Duke of Beaufort Avenue
('Leoforos Dhoukos Bofor') ascends below the Atlantis Hotel to
PLATEIA ELEVTHERIAS and the **Archaeological Museum** (see below). In
the huge square the town takes the air in the early evening; cafés extend
into the roadway and below the trees, where all the birds of Herakleion
roost at sunset; on Sunday the city band plays in the bandstand.
Opposite the museum the road for E. Crete descends through the walls
where stood St George's Gate (Porta del Lazzareto), built in 1565. An
old fountain survives in the wall on the left of the road and a statue of
Venizelos is prominent on the bastion above to the right. Opposite this,
along the higher road, the *Mina Yeoryiadhi Park* extends along the
ramparts with walks of exotic trees.

From the Plateia, LEOFOROS VAS. KONSTANDINOU, with good
confectioners and jewellers, passes down to the town centre. This avenue
approximately follows the southern limit of the Saracen and Byzantine
town; the digging of foundations for modern houses revealed traces of
the rampart of this period. The government offices on the left of the
street occupy Turkish buildings on the site of Venetian barracks. The N.
gate of the courts' block, formerly part of a Franciscan monastery, was
sent from Rome by Pope Alexander V. Steps between the courts lead
past a Statue of Dhaskaloyannis to the Post Office.

On reaching PLATEIA NIKEPHOROU PHOKA, once just 'the place where
the traffic policeman stands' (he sometimes stands there still, but only to
see that the traffic lights are obeyed), we are only a few paces S. of Plat.
Venizelou, our starting-point. To the left runs Odhos 1866, the lively
food market of the town. The first street off this to the left consists of
small taverns. At the top, beyond the market, stands the *Bembo
Fountain* (built in 1588) of antique fragments. It stands behind a
polygonal kiosk, now a shop, adapted from a Turkish fountain. We are
now at the N. side of PLATEIA KORNAROU. From the square, Evans St.
continues up to pass through the walls at the *Kainouria Porta* (New
Gate) dated 1567–87. The passage through the gate shows the walls to be
45 yds thick. The road to the right within the walls leads to the
Martinengo Bastion (view) on which is the tomb of Nikos Kazantzakis,
the author, who died in 1957 in Germany. The inscription reads "I hope

for nothing. I fear nothing. I am free."

From Plateia Nikephorou Phoka (see above) a main shopping street, Kalokairinou, once the Venetian 'Via Imperialis', runs out to the *Porta Khanion* (Khania or Panigra Gate), built c. 1570 (now restored); beyond it are the Phaistos and Tylissos bus terminals. A short way along Kalokairinou any of the little streets to the left leads to Plateia Ayia Aikaterini (St Catherine's Square), named after the church of AYIA AIKATERINI, which was built in 1555 but altered in the 17C. The Mt Sinai monastery of St Catherine had a centre here in the adjacent Ayioi Dheka during the Cretan renaissance (16–17C; comp. p. 13). The Basilica (open 10–1, 5–7; fee) contains a collection of ikons and ecclesiastical relics from various churches. Most interesting are the six *Icons by the great 16C master, Mikhailis Dhamaskinos. He was an older contemporary of El Greco and studied and painted in Italy as well as Crete. The icons date from c. 1580–90 and were brought from the church at Valsamonero (see p. 67) to Ayios Minas. They are the Last Supper, the Council of Nicaea (1591), the Adoration of the Magi, Noli me tangere, the Burning Bush and the Mass. There are also fragments of earlier frescoes (in the N. transept) and silver-bound gospels (S. transept). The square is now dominated by the *Cathedral* (1862–95), dedicated to Ayios Minas and one of the largest churches in Greece. Just below stands the smaller church of *Ayios Minas*, built in the 18C.

B   THE HISTORICAL MUSEUM

The *Historical Museum of Crete, opposite the Xenia Hotel, occupies the family house of Andreas Kalokairinos, a notable benefactor of Herakleion, who gave it for the collection.

ADMISSION 9–1, 3–5.30 or 6; 40 dr.; closed Sunday. The rooms are not at present numbered, and the former numbers given below may be modified.

The front entrance gives on to the main floor while the back (in use in 1979) gives on to the basement.

BASEMENT. ROOM 1. Early Christian and Byzantine Period. 6C sculptures from the basilica of Ayios Titos at Gortyn (see p. 68); Byzantine stone well-heads; relief plaques; 6–9C Byzantine tombstones. The doorway to Room 2 is from a Venetian building of Candia (Herakleion).

ROOM 2. Venetian Period. Above the doorway is a relief plaque with the Lion of St Mark (comp. that on the harbour fortress). Left: tombstone dated 1605; along the wall are architectural fragments from the loggia (1626–28), now rebuilt in the town (see p. 34); doorway with double arches from a Venetian house; above the doorway a Venetian frieze and a coat of arms with a lion and a Hebrew inscription of a Jewish family living in Crete in 16C; in front of the doorway is an elaborate fountain from a Venetian palace and between the two windows the arms of the Venetian family of Capello. Along the right-hand wall are other Venetian arms; one of the 15C with a tower, a cross, and a griffin and an inscription in Latin and Armenian (used as a tombstone in the Armenian Church of Candia). The doorway with double arches leads to a small room containing fragments from the Venetian Church of St Francis, destroyed in the earthquake of 1856: part of a Gothic rose-window and a relief representing an angel.—ROOM 4. Turkish Period. Inscriptions, tombstones of governors and other notable citizens, and glazed porcelain tiles from an 18C mosque in the town.

FIRST FLOOR. ENTRANCE HALL. Fresco painting from the Venetian church of the Madonna dei Crociferi in Herakleion; prow of a Venetian galley. In the corridor (Room 3) from the hall are tombstones and inscriptions in Greek and Latin from the Venetian period. ROOM 5. Early Christian and Byzantine Antiquities. Oil lamps, bronze crucifixes, candlesticks, bronze objects (6C) from the basilica of Ayios Titos at Gortyn and 14C and 15C fresco fragments from Cretan churches.— ROOM 6. Left: icons of 1655 from the monastery of Savathiana, including the Virgin and the Prophets and St Peter and St Paul, the descent from the Cross and the Virgin between two angels (the latter from the Armenian Church of St John). At the end of the room is a painted Crucifix from the Church of the Panayia Gouverniótissa. On the wall to the right of the entrance: late 16C to early 17C fresco fragments from the Church of the Gouverniótissa Pedhiadhos and the Potamies monastery. Note also the remains of a 16C wooden iconostasis. On each side of the entrance are glass cases with 16–17C pottery. Two other cases contain exhibits from the Asomatos Monastery (Rethymno Province), vestments, crucifixes, Gospels, and other liturgical objects. Other cases contain coins from the Byzantine, Venetian, and Turkish periods and Byzantine and Venetian jewellery and seals.—ROOM 7. Documents and other objects relating to Cretan insurrections during the Turkish period. Also on this floor is a reconstructed Byzantine *Chapel*.

SECOND FLOOR. ROOM 8. Manuscripts (10–19C) including Venetian maps and plans.—ROOM 9 is furnished as the study of Nikos Kazantzakis (1883–1957). It contains his desk, his library, editions and translations of his novels, photographs, and various personal possessions.—ROOM 10 represents the living-room in the house of a Cretan peasant of about 1900.—ROOM 11. Exhibition of Cretan and Aegean dresses and woven fabrics. A large room displays material concerning the Cretan statesman M. Tsouderos (1817–77), and another shows photographs of the Battle of Crete (1941).

C THE ARCHAEOLOGICAL MUSEUM

The **Archaeological Museum**, off Plateia Eleftherias, contains a vast collection of material of all periods of Cretan history from Neolithic to Roman, amassed since 1883. A functional building of surpassing external ugliness designed on anti-seismic principles in 1937–40, it is internally spacious, airy, and light. The arrangement and display are superb. At least two visits should be made, preferably before and after the sites have been seen.

Open Apr-May weekdays 8-1, 3–5, Sun and hol from 10; Jun–mid-Oct 8–6.30; winter 9–1, 3–6, Sun and hol 10–1. Closed Tuesdays. Adm 50 dr.; free on Thurs and Sundays.

A detailed Guide Book in English by S. Alexiou, with an introduction by N. Platon (1968), is available.—Qualified guides may be hired to conduct parties or individuals round (charge agreed beforehand).

The case-numbering of the lower floor rooms starts with the right-hand wall as

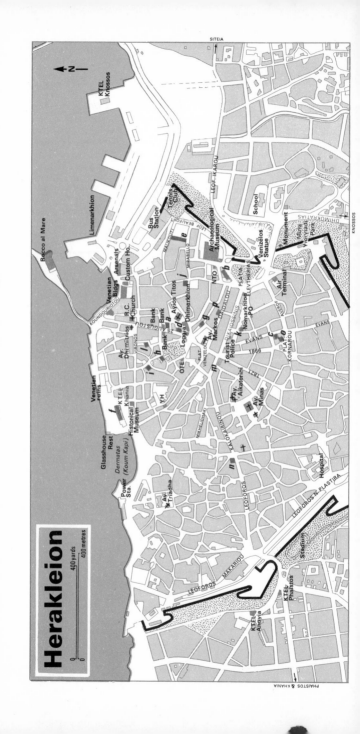

you enter, goes round the room anti-clockwise and ends in the centre. Our description sometimes diverges from exact case order.

GALLERY 1. NEOLITHIC AND MINOAN PREPALATIAL CIVILIZATION (early Minoan). Cases 1 & 2 contain Neolithic and Sub-Neolithic pottery, violin-shaped and steatopygous idols, and bone and stone implements from Knossos, the cave of Eileithyia near Amnisos, Phourni in E. Crete, Phaistos and other sites. Note the white-filled incised decoration of the Neolithic pottery and the red-incrusted decoration of that from Phaistos.—Case 3 illustrates from burial caves the various styles of 'Sub-Neolithic' or Early Minoan I (3000–2400 B.C.) with grey wares and pattern-burnished vases from Partira (S. of Knossos) and Pyrgos (at Nirou Khani on the N. coast E. of Herakleion) and red on buff-painted wares from the cave of Kyparissi near Kanli Kastelli. Note the round bottoms typical of these E.M. I vases.—Case 4 is devoted to Early Minoan vases from the tholos tombs at Lebena, especially the E.M. I red on buff and white on red wares in a great profusion of shapes. Also from Lebena (Case 5) are jewellery, figurines, and bronze daggers.

Case 6 contains E.M. II Vasilike mottled ware, in particular jugs and long spouted teapots; these are from Vasilike (upper shelves) and other E. Cretan sites (bottom shelf). In Case 7 the finest of the early stone vases come from Mochlos (E.M. II–III, 2600–2100 B.C.). It is interesting to see how well the banded marbles and limestones are adapted to the shapes of the vases. Breccia, chlorite and polished green serpentine, and black and creamy steatite are also used. The vases were made by hand, the inside being cut out with a reed or copper drill with an abrasive powder to do the cutting. The lid of a pyxis with a dog handle and a fine large chlorite pyxis with incised decoration (from Maronia) are noteworthy.—Case 8 displays Early Minoan III vases from Vasilike and Mochlos. A style with white decoration on a dark ground (black or brown) now replaces the Vasilike mottled ware but many of the earlier shapes continue. Cases 9 & 10 contain vases from the Mesara tombs, including a bronze basin from Kalathiana and E.M.–M.M. I vases from Palaikastro in E. Crete. Note the small boat, also the four-wheeled cart, the earliest evidence for wheeled transport from Crete (c. 2000 B.C.).

In centre: Case 11. Early and Middle Minoan I sealstones from the Mesara, notably the ivory cylinders with designs cut at each end (see also 1098, the Babylonian haematite cylinder of the period of Hammurabi). Cases 12–15. E.M. pottery from Koumasa, including bird-shaped vases, and Middle Minoan bulls with tiny acrobats clinging to the horns, and from Ayios Onouphrios, white marble and limestone figurines of Cycladic type; sealstones from Central and E. Crete (especially the cave of Trapeza and Mochlos; four-sided prisms are popular and some have signs in the Hieroglyphic script), flat, leaf-shaped daggers and longer ones with a central midrib (three from Koumasa and one from near Viannos are of silver, the remainder of copper and bronze) and stone vessels from the Mesara tombs, especially bird's nest bowls and square and rectangular vases with four or two cups and incised decoration on the sides.—In Case 16 and the central Cases (17, and 18A) are displayed elegant gold, rock crystal, and carnelian jewellery and necklaces, among them gold chains with minute links, from Mochlos and the Mesara tombs, while Case 18 has further sealstones.

GALLERY II. MINOAN PROTOPALATIAL CIVILIZATION (M.M. I–II). This room is devoted mainly to finds of this period from **Knossos** and **Mallia**. In Case 19 are the earliest vases from the Mallia Palace and cemeteries, including some mottled E.M. II Vasilike ware; notice also the moulds for double axes and the stone vases from the cemeteries.— Case 20. M.M. I pottery from the rectangular burial enclosures at Gournes, E. of Herakleion, then (continuing in Case 21) a series of clay figurines. A pithos burial in the corner shows a typical method of interment in this period. Case 21B. Seals from recent excavations on Mt Juktas. Cases 22 & 23. Pottery from houses below the West Court of Knossos, then fine polychrome Middle Minoan I–II vases from Knossos.Between these cases are several clay burial chests (larnakes). Case 24 contains M.M. I figurines from the peak sanctuary of Petsofa, above Palaikastro at the eastern end of Crete. Note the elaborate head-dresses of the female figures and the daggers worn in their belts by the males. There are also three figurines from a house at Khamaizi in E. Crete as well as a clay model shrine with doves perched on the pillars, from Knossos. The central case (25) nearest the entrance to the room contains the polychrome faience plaques from Knossos, known as the Town Mosaic since they are models of Middle Minoan house façades, sometimes three stories high. This case also contains tablets, labels, and bars in the M.M. hieroglyphic script, and a gold-hilted dagger (recent find from Mallia).—Case 26. Characteristic pottery from Mallia and bronze cauldrons; the other central cases (27–29) contain Middle Minoan seals and polychrome pottery including large vessels from Knossos. Note (in 29) the pithos decorated with palm trees.

GALLERY III. Same period. Here (Case 30) are the polychrome vases from the Kamares cave, which gave Kamares ware its name, and the remainder of the room is devoted to the astonishing collection of *Vases and other objects from the **First Palace of Phaistos**. Popular shapes are bridge-spouted jars and several forms of cup, many with thin, metallic-like carinated profiles. Many of these vases and those from Knossos in the previous room show a wonderful harmony between the design and the shape, the patterns being carefully adapted to the form of the vase. Some of the smaller vases are known as eggshell ware because of the incredible thinness of their walls. Of the larger vessels a tall vase with attached white flowers and a fruitstand or bowl with elaborately painted interior (both in Case 43) are noteworthy. The central case (42) displays the contents of a shrine from a room bordering the W. Court at Phaistos. Notice the great red-burnished clay libation table with border decoration of oxen and spiral designs. In Case 41 is the famous *Phaistos Disk, with stamped characters in an unknown Hieroglyphic script. The words are divided by incised lines and the inscription runs from the outside to the centre. The disk was found in a room of M.M. III date (17C B.C.).

GALLERY IV. NEOPALATIAL CIVILIZATION (Middle Minoan III to Late Minoan I). In case 44 from Knossos are two conical clay cups with ink inscriptions in the Linear A script. From Knossos also (in Case 45) come the vases with spiral decoration and others with white lilies on the dark ground. Case 46. Vessels used in worship of the Sacred Snake. On the opposite side of the room, in Cases 47–48, finds from the Palace and houses of Mallia, notably the brown schist sceptre, one end a leopard, the other an axe, a series of domestic vessels and lamps in clay and stone, and several bronze utensils. The finds (Case 49) from the final destruction of the Palace of Phaistos in Late Minoan I B, c. 1450 B.C., were few, but notice the graceful jug with grasses all over and a rhyton decorated with argonauts.—Case 50 contains the smaller finds from the M.M. III Temple Repositories at Knossos: the *Snake Goddess and her votaries, the flying fish and other decorative plaques, all these in faience, banded limestone and marble libation vases, a rock crystal rosette for inlay, and painted shells. In three corners of the room are large vessels of serpentine from Knossos.

The central cases contain some of the finest products of the Minoan civilization. Case 51. The **Bull's Head Rhyton (so called because of the holes in the mouth and head through which sacred libations were poured) is from the Little Palace at Knossos. It is made of serpentine, the eyes inlaid with jasper, rock crystal, and white tridacna shell, the horns (restored) of gilded wood. In Case 57 is the royal *Draughtboard or gaming table, inlaid with ivory, rock crystal, faience, lapis lazuli and gold and silver foil. It was found in a corridor of the Palace at Knossos and is dated c. 1600 B.C. Case 56. Ivory acrobats, probably covered with gold leaf originally. The main figure is in the act of leaping over a bull. Of the other cases, 55 contains bronze scales or balance, and lead and stone weights from various sites, on one side, and on the other faience reliefs, including a very naturalistic cow suckling her calf and a marble cross from the Knossos Temple Repositories; Case 54 contains the large vases from the Repositories including the bird amphoras imported from the Cycladic Islands; adjacent in Case 58 are the stone ritual vessels from the Shrine Treasury of the Palace at Knossos. These are mostly rhytons in alabaster, banded limestones, and other variegated stones.—From the same Treasury came the Lioness Head Rhyton made of a white marble-like limestone. This has Case 59 to itself.—A splendid series of bronzes from houses at Knossos is displayed in Case 53. These include a large saw, a tripod cauldron and bowls with chased decoration of leaves round the rims.

Beside the bronzes is Case 52 with a ceremonial *Sword and other weapons from Mallia, of Middle Minoan date. The sword, nearly a metre long, has a pommel of rock crystal on an ivory hilt. Another sword has a pommel of gold leaf on which is an acrobat. Other finds in this case include stone vase fragments with relief decoration from Knossos (the Ambushed Octopus) and Phaistos and miniature works in ivory, rock crystal, and faience.

GALLERY V. KNOSSOS. THE FINAL PALACE PERIOD (Late Minoan II-IIIA, 1450–1400 B.C.). Around the walls are a series of Palace Style amphoras, some from the Palace, others from the Little Palace and Royal Villa. It may be noticed how a formal element has entered into the decoration, in contrast to the naturalism of the Late Minoan I vases. On the right as we enter is a giant unfinished stone amphora from the Palace with a decoration of shallow spirals. Cases 60 & 61 contain Late Minoan vases from the Knossos Royal Road excavations, architectural fragments from the Palace, stone friezes with split rosettes and spirals in relief, a large stone jug in banded limestone and a ewer of breccia imitating basketwork, clay vases from the Little Palace and silver vessels from the S. House.—Case 62 contains several fine large stone vases and lamps from Knossos made from a reddish marble, antico rosso, imported from the southern Peloponnese. Above are Egyptian finds from Knossos. including an alabaster lid with a cartouche of the Hyksos king Khyan, a large Pre-dynastic or early Dynastic bowl, carinated bowls (Fourth Dynasty) of diorite with a Minoan obsidian imitation, and a diorite statuette of an Egyptian, perhaps an ambassador, called User (Twelfth or early Thirteenth Dynasty). In the last wall case (64) vases dateable to c. 1400–1380 B.C. from the destruction debris of the Palace.

In the central cases are (Case 69) Linear A tablets from Ayia Triadha, Tylissos, Phaistos, Zakro, Palaikastro, and Gournia; Linear B tablets from the Knossos archives; (Case 65) some exquisite Late Minoan sealstones; (Case 66) stone vases from the Palace including the big flat gypsum alabastrons found in the Throne Room, also a bull rhyton of painted clay; (Case 70) various ivories of very fine workmanship; and (Cases 67 & 68) Palace Style octopus amphoras and one of Late Minoan IB date, c. 1450 B.C., for contrast (naturalistic, not degenerate like the others) from the recent Knossos excavations, and select sherds from Knossos, including some from Palace Style vases.

GALLERY VI. NEOPALATIAL CEMETERIES (Middle Minoan III-Late Minoan III, C. 1650–1350 B.C.). Case 71 contains Late Minoan vases from the tholos tomb, used uninterruptedly from Middle Minoan I, at Kamilari S.W. of Phaistos. With them is a most interesting clay shrine with divinities and worshippers. The bird alabastrons are painted in a lively style of c. 1400 B.C. Case 72. Material from the Temple Tomb at Knossos and the Royal Tomb at Isopata. From the latter is the splendid series of Egyptian Eighteenth Dynasty alabaster *Vases and an Old Kingdom bowl in porphyry. Vases of clay and stone from the Knossian cemeteries of Mavro Spelio and Zapher Papoura follow in Case 73, with a Kourotrophos figurine; then Case 74 for a chamber tomb from the rich cemetery at Katsamba, the harbour town of Knossos on the E. side of Herakleion. Also from this tomb group (Case 79A by the far door) is an ivory *Pyxis with a bull-catching scene akin to that on the gold cups from Vapheio (Athens, National Museum). Next comes Case 75 with bronze vessels and utensils from the Tomb of the Tripod Hearth at Zapher Papoura, and above, similar objects from the tholos tomb at Arkhanes.Case 75A contains a sacrificial bull burial.

Beyond, wall cases (76 & 77) display clay and stone vases from tombs at Isopata, including the Tomb of the Double Axes, from the Late Minoan II Warrior Graves under the Sanatorium N. of Knossos and from another tomb of this date from Knossos. In Case 78, a reconstructed boar's tusk *Helmet from the Zapher Papoura cemetery (a Mycenean import ?). The remaining wall case (79) contains stone lamps and vases including some of Egyptian alabaster as well as imported Eighteenth Dynasty alabastrons, clay vases (notice the bird alabastrons), and an imported glass bottle, all from the Late Minoan cemetery at Kalyvia near Phaistos.

The central cases contain amphoras from the Royal Tomb at Isopata; (Case 82) large stone vessels from the Katsamba cemetery including an Egyptian alabaster vase with a cartouche of Thutmosis III (1504–1450 B.C.), the great king of the Eighteenth Dynasty, and a Late Minoan II amphora showing helmets with cheek-pieces. Case 80. Libation jug from

Katsamba with stylized argonauts and spiked decoration. Cases 81, 86 & 87 contain jewellery and ivory toilet articles from the Phaistos and Knossos cemeteries, and from various other tombs. Particularly fine (in Case 87) is the gold *Ring with a dancing divinity and worshippers from Isopata, and earrings in the shape of bulls' heads, done in the granulation technique. Case 88 contains finds from tholos tombs at Arkhanes, including jewellery, a bronze mirror with an ivory handle and a pyxis lid in ivory with figure-eight shield handles. Cases 84 & 85 contain weapons from Mycenean warrior graves near Knossos with a bronze *Helmet equipped with cheek-pieces..

GALLERY VII. NEOPALATIAL SETTLEMENTS OF CENTRAL AND SOUTH CRETE (Late Minoan I, c. 1550-1450 B.C.). The first objects on the right are large bronze double axes set up on restored poles and painted bases. These are from the villa of Nirou Khani on the coast E. of Herakleion. This building contained other cult objects such as painted plaster tripod tables and stone horns of consecration. Case 89. Bronze figurines of male worshippers, vases, and stone lamps, from Nirou Khani and finds from the villas at Tylissos, including a rhyton of dark grey imported obsidian, extremely difficult to carve because of its hardness and liability to fracture. In Case 90 vases from the villas at Amnisos, Sklavokambos, and Vathypetro. Notice the fine bridge-spouted jug with zig-zag patterns and the stone concial rhyton from Sklavokambos. The stone lamps and large cup (second and lower shelves) are from Vathypetro, the vases and head on the upper shelf from Amnisos. The opposite wall cases (91 & 93) contain vases from the two Minoan houses at Prasa, a little E. of Herakleion, and from Ayia Triadha, the latter including several of the Marine Style. Carbonized beans, barley, millet, and figs from Phaistos and Palaikastro are also shown. In between, Case 92, bronze figurines and small votive animals from the Dictaean Cave and other cave sites.

Separately displayed in the small central cases are the three famous serpentine relief vases from Ayia Triadha: the *Chieftain Cup (95), the *Boxer Vase (96), and the **Harvester Vase (94), often considered the finest product of Minoan art. Each portrays scenes from the daily life of the Minoans. The other cases contain (97) bronze weapons from the votive cave at Arkalokhori; bronze figurines and ivory rosettes from Tylissos and a bronze figure from Grivigla near Rethymno; and (98) the hoard of votive double axes from the Arkalokhori cave. Case 99. Copper talents or ox-hide ingots (weight 64 lb), incised with Minoan signs, and copper hammers from Ayia Triadha; (102) human and animal votive offerings from the same site, stone vases, including a beautiful dolium shell of white-spotted obsidian and a Hittite sphinx; (100) bronze tools, utensils and jewellery, all from Ayia Triadha, two potter's wheels from Vathypetro and seals from various sites. Along one wall are three huge bronze cauldrons from Tylissos.

Standing on their own are various large vessels, including a huge stone basin from Ayia Triadha. Two coarse limestone thrones are from Katsamba and Prinias. In the central Case 101, gold and silver jewellery from Central and E. Crete. There are several examples with granulation. Here also is one of the great treasures of Minoan art, the gold *Pendant of M.M.I date from the Khrysolakkos cemetery at Mallia. It consists of two conjoined bees (or wasps or hornets) around a golden ball with a smaller ball within, covered with granulation.

GALLERY VIII. THE PALACE OF ZAKRO (Late Minoan I, c. 1550–1450 B.C.). The wall cases (103–110) are mainly devoted to clay vases found in the Palace. These include a series of plain flower vases with high curving handles, a fruitstand with spiral decoration, Marine Style vases, and a large ritual jug; (109) an exquisite rock crystal *Rhyton with a handle of beads turned green by the bronze wire on which they are threaded. There are also white limestone libation tables and a stone column capital. Case III contains the *Peak Sanctuary Rhyton, a magnificent vase showing in relief a mountain shrine with wild goats, plants, and flowers. A few traces survive of the gold leaf which once covered it. Case 116 holds a bull's head *Rhyton, made of chlorite. It is smaller than that from Knossos but of equally fine workmanship. Other cases display (117) objects of faience, including a large argonaut and butterflies; (122) a large double axe with chased decoration (see the restored drawing on the wall); (113) a huge burnt ivory tusk said to be imported from Syria, bronze ingots, and several very fine Late Minoan IB vases; (115) bronzes including long swords and a huge saw; and, in two cases (114 & 118) the magnificent series of *Stone vessels, mostly from the Shrine Treasury.

These comprise conical and fluted rhytons of Egyptian alabaster and polychrome banded limestones, one also of lapis Lacedaemonius (a stone imported from near Sparta), a group of chalices including examples in gabbro, white-spotted obsidian, and polychrome limestones, two Old Kingdon Egyptian vases in porphyritic rock adapted for use by the Minoans, several individual vases made of Egyptian alabaster and an Eighteenth Dynasty imported alabastron, and a large multiple vase with high curving handles and made of polychrome banded limestone. This case also contains three stone hammers and two faience animal head rhytons.—Free-standing in the room are large pithoi including one (in the centre) with a Linear A inscription.

GALLERY IX. NEOPALATIAL SETTLEMENTS OF EAST CRETE (Late Minoan I, c. 1700–1450 B.C.). The finds are from the settlements of Palaikastro, Mokhlos, Gournia, Pseira, and Zakro. Cases 119 & 120 on the right are devoted to Palaikastro. The first contains stone vases and lamps, one of antico rosso with ivy scrolls on the columns. Notice also a clay bull rhyton and bronze figurines, the large one from Praisos. The second case contains three fine L.M. IB vases including an octopus flask and a jug with papyrus decoration, and two clay cat's heads. Between these two cases Case 161 displays unpublished finds from Myrtos. The central case (125) opposite has Marine Style rhytons, a gabbro rhyton and stone libation tables from Palaikastro. In case 121 (opposite wall) are a series of L.M. I vases from Gournia (an octopus stirrup vase in its own case), a small bull's head rhyton, and a bronze figurine, and, in Case 122, clay and stone vases and lamps from Pseira, with a magnificent rhyton of breccia. The remaining wall-case (123) contains, from the M.M.-L.M.I peak sanctuary at Piskokefalo near Siteia, clay votives, human and animal, beetles (rhinoceros oryctes) being the most common. Sometimes they have climbed on to the human figures.

In the central cases are (124) clay sealings from Knossos, Ayia Triadha, Zakro, and Sklavokambos, one from Knossos showing two personages with a Hieroglyphic inscription, perhaps a title, beside them, together with small objects, notably ivories and inlays, from Palaikastro and other E. Cretan sites; (128) an unparalleled collection of Late Minoan *Sealstones in agate, carnelian, chalcedony, jasper, lapis

Lacedaemonius, lapis lazuli, rock crystal, and other stones, from many sites. The main shapes are the lentoid, amygdaloid (almond shape), and flattened cylinder. Particularly noteworthy are Nos. 1656–9 from the Knossos Warrior Graves, 165–80 from the Kalyvia cemetery at Phaistos, as well as those in lapis lazuli from Knossos.

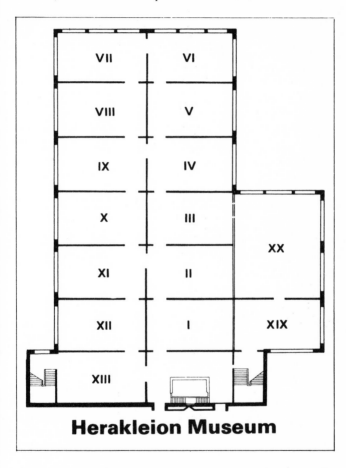

Herakleion Museum

Beyond stands Case 129 with finds from Mokhlos, clay vases, bull rhytons, a stone lamp with foliate band decoration, and bronze vessels including a cup with chased ivy decoration, closely similar in shape to the gold cups from Vapheio in Athens. Finds from Gournia are opposite in Case 126. There are many rhytons and a fine fluted stone example in antico rosso, and several very large low lamps of limestone. Case 127 contains a large series of bronze tools, utensils, and weapons, mostly from Gournia with a few from the other E. Cretan sites. Around the room are several large vases from E. Crete including burial pithoi from the cemetery of Pakhyammos just E. of Gournia.

GALLERY X. POSTPALATIAL PERIOD (Late Minoan III, 1350–1100 B.C.). The decline in the Minoan culture is reflected in the remains of the post-palatial age. It is noticeable how vase-painting has lost its vitality. Fine stonework no longer occurs. Most of the material exhibited is from tombs for there has as yet been little preserved from settlements of this period. Wall cases (130 & 131) on the right exhibit L.M. III pottery from Phoinikia, Katsamba, Phaistos, Gournia, and Palaikastro. Popular shapes are the high-stemmed kylix, tankard, ladle, krater, and stirrup vase. the earlier L.M. patterns have now become stylized, but the bird decoration of the first part of L.M. III is interesting—Case 132. From Palaikastro comes the group of figures dancing round a musician playing the lyre. The single wall case (133) contains large clay idols with raised arms from Gazi, W. of Herakleion. The central figure may be a goddess since she has a head-dress of poppies. Case 134 & 136 display pottery from L.M. III chamber tombs at Episkope and Stamnioi, Pedhiadha, S.E. of Herakleion (notice also the serpentine vase with five receptacles), and from Episkope near Hierapetra and Mouliana in E. Crete. From Episkope come several fine flattened stirrup vases and from Mouliana a large flask decorated with concentric circles and Close Style stirrup vases with octopus decoration. In Case 135, between the two last, are votive figurines from Kannia, near Gortyn. In Case 137 are tomb groups from Amnisos (Karteros), Gournes and Pakhyammos. The imported glass bottle is from Amnisos and the limestone horns of consecration from Porós, the eastern suburb of Herakleion. Case 138 contains life-like horses and riders.

The central cases contain the following objects: (139) bead necklaces, mostly of glass paste, some of semi-precious stones, from the tombs at Gournes, Episkope and Stamnioi, Pedhiadha, and Milatos, together with stone moulds for ornaments; (140) finds from L.M. III shrines at Knossos (Shrine of the Double Axes), Phaistos and Gournia, with clay huts also from the first two sites; (141) large vases, especially kraters, from Mouliana (one with a warrior on horseback), Phaistos and Knossos; (142) contents of shrines from Gournia, Prinias (Sub-Minoan), Koumasa in the Mesara and Kalo Khorio Pedhaidha (the head of a large idol); (143) clay idols, animals and human, from sanctuaries at Ayia Triadha (notice especially the figure on a swing) and the cave of Hermes in the gorge of Patsos; (144) tools and weapons of all kinds in bronze, the main series from the two L.M. IIIc tombs at Mouliana in E. Crete.

GALLERY XI. SUB-MINOAN AND GEOMETRIC PERIOD. 1100–650 B.C. The wall cases on the right (145, 146, 147) contain, in the first, Protogeometric and Geometric vases from Phaistos (upper shelf) and from the large cemetery at Kourtes, including a kernos with alternating cups and figurines; in the second, vases of this period from Kavousi and Vrokastro in E. Crete with a basket vase (kalathos), a horse figurine and a bronze tripod; and in the third, Geometric vases and bronze figurines from sites in Central and E. Crete, Psykhro, Ay. Triadha, Ay. Syllas, Amnisos, Kavousi, and Vrokastro. In the adjacent central case (154) are clay vases and ritual objects, including clay huts, from the L.M. IIIc mountain refuge settlement at Karphi above Lasithi. The Model of a house sanctuary is from a Protogeometric tomb at Teke, between Herakleion and Knossos. The large clay idols from Karphi are exhibited in the single wall case (148). The one with sacred symbols on her head may be a goddess. With these is a peculiar rhyton in the form of a charioteer drawn by bulls, of which only the heads are shown. Continuing round, we find in Case 149 objects from the cave of Eileithyia at Inatos on the S. coast. These include clay figures embracing (? copulating) and pregnant women (Eileithyia was the goddess of childbirth), model boats and double axes. Case 150 and the two adjacent central cases (156 & 157) contain a large series of vases from Geometric tombs at Teke. In Case 151 are finds from the rich tombs recently dug at Prinias, where gold shields with swastikas and a 'star of David' pendant make to the anachronistic eye a strange juxtaposition. The remaining central case (158) on this side has small finds from the Inatos cave, including an ivory figurine of a naked goddess, faience goddesses, scarabs, necklaces, jewellery, ornaments, and votives. The central case (153) opposite exhibits iron and bronze tools, weapons, utensils, pins, fibulae and tweezers from various sites including Knossos, Kourtes, Kavousi, Vrokastro, Arkhades, and Praisos. An empty case (152) awaits arrangement.

GALLERY XII. GEOMETRIC AND ARCHAIC PERIODS. 8–7C B.C. In this room is a large series of Geometric burial urns from tombs in the Knossos area, especially near Fortetsa, and from the Arkades (Aphrati) cemetery in Central Crete. Note the unusual polychrome decoration of the Knossian vases, with patterns of lilies, papyri, and rosettes. The miniature vases on the lids of some urns were offerings for the dead. Smaller vases show Orientalizing and Protocorinthian influence. The vases from the Arkhades cemetery (Case 168) are also Geometric and Orientalizing. Human and mythical figures and scenes are shown and there is also a series of plastic figures, human and animal. Imported vases are from Rhodes and Corinth. In the central case (170) is a magnificent collection of 8–7C *Jewellery, mainly from a tomb at Teke. This treasure includes a snake-chain necklace, with a gold pendant, a rock-crystal necklace and silver pins with gold heads ornamented with birds. The techniques of inlay, granulation, and filigree are all used. There is also a series of gold and electrum dumps, considered among the earliest examples of Greek coinage. The Mistress of Animals is represented between two companions on a gold sheet from the Idaian cave and there is also miniature gold-work from Arkades, Knossos, and Praisos. In the two central cases (164 & 169) opposite the relief pithoi are a decorated bronze girdle from Fortetsa, fragments of relief pithoi, fragments of a bronze tripod decorated with relief scenes, from the Idaian cave, wheel-handles of tripod cauldrons and an embossed bronze quiver with sphinxes and a hero fighting lions. There is also a pair of bronze greaves from Kavousi. The huge relief pithoi opposite date from Sub-Minoan (from Prinias) to Archaic. That with Orientalizing motives of sphinxes and leopard-headed spirals is from Lyttos, the others from Arkadhes and Dreros.

THE GALLERY OF THE SARCOPHAGI. The Minoans often used clay chests or larnakes for burial purposes. Those displayed here are of two periods: Middle Minoan tub-shaped examples, painted with abstract designs, from various sites including Vóroi in the Mesara. Late Minoan III rectangular chests on four feet, often with gabled lids. Usually the designs on these chests consist of degenerate octopuses, but two examples here are more interesting, an agrimi with its kid on a larnax from Gournia, and that from Palaikastro with religious symbols and an animal with a collar or ruff round its neck. Sometimes elliptical bathtubs with marine designs inside were used for burials, and examples can be seen with a plug-hole to let the water escape. From occasional remains of wood in tombs and the panelled form of the L.M. III chests it is considered that earlier L.M. ones were made of wood.

In one corner of this room can be seen a burial, transported from an L.M. III A–B tomb at Sellopoulo, near Knossos. In another corner is a wooden model reconstruction of the palace at Knossos, made by the late master-technician, Zacharias Kanakes.

GALLERY XIV. HALL OF THE FRESCOES. This is reached by the stairs from the Gallery of the Sarcophagi. Here and in XV and XVI are displayed the **Minoan Frescoes**. Though only fragments of the original wall-paintings and sometimes much burnt, they vividly illustrate the life of the Minoans, especially their interest in animals, plants, and flowers. The surviving pieces are mostly from Knossos and Ayia Triadha; Amnisos, Nirou Khani, Pseira, and Tylissos contribute a few examples. Several of the miniature pieces repay close study. The paintings, with one exception, date from the Neopalatial Period (mainly Late Minoan I, c. 1550–1450 B.C.; some from Knossos are L.M. II–IIIA, c. 1450–1400 B.C.).

The first fragment on the left is a Bull's Foot, from the Upper Hall of the Double Axes at Knossos. Next come the remains of the Procession Fresco and the Cup bearer (notice the seal on his wrist) from the Corridor of the Procession in the Palace. Between the doors, the Griffin Fresco from the Throne Room. Beyond are the fragments from Ayia Triadha: a kneeling female figure, perhaps picking flowers in a garden; a seated goddess; a cat stalking a pheasant in a park—the pheasant struts about, not suspecting danger; a fresco (very similar to one that appears on the sarcophagus in the centre of the room, and probably painted by the same artist), showing a religious procession with a musician leading; a religious composition showing parts of a shrine and worshippers in procession bringing offerings; and a woman and deer in a natural setting. At the end of the room is a floor fresco from a shrine at Ayia Triadha. It consists of a colourful marine scene showing dolphins, an octopus and small fishes. Beyond are the remains of another floor fresco with abstract motives from the First Palace at Phaistos (18C B.C.).

We proceed now from this corner along the S. wall. All save the last two frescoes are from Knossos. First is the restored Shield Fresco from the upper Hall of the Colonnades. The markings on the shields represent the dappled hides of the oxen or bulls from which real shields were made. This work is of the last Palace Period (1450–1400 B.C.) as the rosette spirals show. A very similar Shield Fresco was found in the Palace at Tiryns and, more recently, another at Mycenae. Next comes the Priest King or Prince of the Lilies wearing his plumed lily head-dress and collar of fleurs-de-lis and leading an animal, perhaps a griffin, for this theme is shown on sealstones. The Charging Bull in stucco relief is from the portico above the N. Entrance Passage, the Ladies in Blue from the E. Wing of the Palace and the Dolphins from the Queen's Megaron. There follow two colourful spiral frieze frescoes and then, from the Caravanserai S. of the Palace, the frieze of partridges and hoopoes. The coloured objects are probably stones rather than eggs. Next comes the *Toreador Fresco, the most vivid representation of bull-leaping in

Minoan art. Red is the convention for male figures, white for female, and here we see both participating in this sport. The last two frescoes on the wall are the graceful white and red Madonna lilies and irises from the L.M. I villa at Amnisos. Such lilies are frequently seen today in Cretan gardens. At this end of the hall a central case contains fragments of a chariot fresco and other pieces from Knossos.

In the centre (Case 171) stands the famous painted limestone *Sarcophagus (c. 1400 B.C.) from Ayia Triadha. The long sides portray religious ceremonies with processions of figures bearing offerings and conducting a sacrifice; a figure, probably a dead man, appears at the entrance to what may be his tomb. On the ends are shown chariot groups drawn by horses and winged griffins.

Galleries XV & XVI open off the main fresco hall. All the pieces are from Knossos except where otherwise stated.

In GALLERY XV: the Miniature Fresco from rooms W. of the N. Entrance Passage; crowds of spectators attend some ceremony, including a dance, while another part of the picture shows a shrine with columns which have double axes attached. Next is *'La Parisienne', probably a priestess because of the Sacral Knot over her neck. Beside her is the restored Camp Stool fresco with priests and priestesses sitting on stools holding chalices and goblets. 'La Parisienne' may have been associated with this group though she is much bigger. The Spiral Cornice Relief came from a room W. of the N. Entrance Passage. Next are displayed relief fragments of arms, legs, and a hand, then two griffins tied to a column tail to tail. There seems to have been a whole frieze of these in high relief antithetically grouped in the E. Hall of the Palace above the Corridor of the Bays. The central case in this room contains fragments of miniature style frescoes from Knossos and Tylissos, some from the latter site showing scenes with boxers.

In GALLERY XVI, opposite, further fragments from Knossos are displayed in the central case (174); these include the Palanquin Fresco, part of a bull-leaping scene, pieces of the Miniature Frescoes, shrines, and dress fragments. On the walls we begin in the corner left of entrance from the main hall. First comes the original restoration of the Saffron Gatherer when the main figure was thought to be a boy. Later it was determined that it was a blue monkey, as shown in N. Platon's adjacent restoration. Next comes the Captain of the Blacks, from the area of the L.M. I House of the Frescoes, a dancing girl, from the Queen's Megaron, a tri-columnar shrine (this fragment was found in the W. Magazines of the Palace), and olive trees in relief, from the N. Entrance Passage. On the opposite wall comes first another olive tree in relief, then the Blue Bird and Monkey Frescoes from the House of the Frescoes, women or goddesses in stucco relief, with elaborate dresses, from the island of Pseira and finally a Sacral Knot from the L.M. I villa at Nirou Khani, E. of Herakleion.

GALLERY XVII. THE *GIAMALAKIS COLLECTION. The collection formed over a period of forty years by the late Dr S. Giamalakis, a surgeon of Herakleion, is now displayed in this room. There are many objects of outstanding interest but not all of them were found in Crete: (175) Early and Middle Minoan pottery and a Cycladic 'frying-pan' with incised decoration; a steatopygous burnished Neolithic figurine from Apano Khorio near Ierapetra; (176) over fifty stone vases including some of banded marble like those from Mochlos; a case (187) of Minoan and later seals; another (189) of non-Minoan seals, including cylinder seals and Sassanid bullas made of chalcedony; (178) a bronze figure bearing a ram over its shoulders; (190) a helmet from Axos; (191) a gold treasure from Zakro which includes a diadem with the Mistress of Animals, a gold cup and bull's head; several bronzes; (182) Archaic and Classical Greek terracottas and vases and some very fine Venetian jewellery.

GALLERY XVIII. ARCHAIC TO GRECO-ROMAN ANTIQUITIES. The exhibits in this room consist mainly of terracottas, bronzes and coins from the Archaic, Classical, Hellenistic, and Roman cities of the island.

Cases 192–194 contain: 7C to Classical clay figurines, pottery and plaques from a votive deposit on the acropolis of Gortyn (also Case 200); several figures have the wig-like hairstyle known as 'Dedalic', one figure represents Athena brandishing her spear; in Case 206 the plaques include Bellerophon fighting the Chimaera, and Klytemnestra and Aegisthus killing Agamemnon, while others show Archaic naked or clothed goddesses wearing high polos head-dresses.—Case 195. From Arkades is a Dedalic head-vase (6639), from Praisos a protome of a man with a diadem, from the sanctuary of Zeus Cretagnes at Palaikastro a Gorgoneion (4920); also exhibited are a plaque with a sphinx from Lyttos and several fragments of Archaic relief pithoi. Cases 196, 197, 203 & 207A contain fine bronzes from Axos, Dreros, the acropolis of Gortyn, the Idaian cave and Praisos. These include mitrai (armour to protect the abdomen) from Axos, with incised decoration, one showing Pegasus, another a tripod between two lions, a third two contending runners; a bronze corselet from Arkades (197), a Gorgoneion and a Palladion from Dreros; numerous handle attachments from the Idaian cave; and miniature votive armour from the sanctuaries of Praisos and Gortyn. Small clay figurines of the Archaic period, human and animal, come from Amnisos, Tylissos, and the Idaian cave, and (in Case 198) embossed and cast bronze helmets and vases from Axos, the Idaian cave and Teke between Herakleion and Knossos. A vase from Dreros, standing separately, is decorated with a wild goat and snakes in relief.

Case 205, The Classical and Hellenistic coins of Crete are mostly of bronze and silver. Rare gold coins from Lissos and Hyrtakina in S.W. Crete are also shown here. There are coins based on the Attic tetradrachm with the names of Cretan archons. Greek silver coins of Athens, Aegina, Argos, Corinth, and Sikyon, and coins of Macedon and the Hellenistic monarchies are also shown. (The Roman coins of Crete are in the Study Collection.)

Case 199 is devoted to Greek black- and red-figure vases; these include a good red-figure lekythos from Kydonia (Khania), Classical lamps and terracottas, Attic, and Boeotian vases (not from Crete). Cases 201 & 202, Hellenistic vases including several Gnathian examples with plant motives on a light or dark ground, Hellenistic white marble pyxides, Greco-Roman bronzes, terracottas, lamps and glass vessels. Among these are Late Roman bronze and clay lamps with erotic relief scenes. There are also several small Greco-Roman heads in marble.

Case 207 containing Classical, Hellenistic, and Roman jewellery and gems includes a fine Victory, from Knossos, inspired by the Victory of Paionios at Olympia, ear-rings from Olous, diadems and a series of gold and silver rings. Among the gems is one of onyx with a representation of a Centaur, another of chalcedony with Theseus and the Minotaur.

Beside the curtained door to the Study Collection is a life-size bronze
*Statue of a boy in sandals and toga from Ierapetra. It is a most sensitive
portrayal of the 1C B.C.

GROUND FLOOR. GALLERY XIX. ARCHAIC SCULPTURES AND BRONZES
700–550 B.C. Above the entrance is a 7C Gorgoneion from Dreros. In the
corner to the left there is a lion head in poros from Phaistos and up on
the wall to the left a frieze of horsemen from one of the two mid-7C
temples at Prinias (ancient Ryzenia). Below this frieze are two groups of
Archaic sculpture from the acropolis of Gortyn, one representing a god
embracing two goddesses, the other three goddesses. Also on this side
are two funerary stelai from Gortyn, a warrior and a lady spinning.
Above the door to Gallery XX are the seated goddesses from the
doorway leading into the cella of one of the Prinias temples. Their
thrones are placed over a frieze of lions and deer, suggesting that the
divinity may be the Cretan Britomartis (Artemis), Mistress of Animals.
Also exhibited on the left side of the room are an eagle and a hawk on
pedestals with Ionic volutes, from the sanctuary of Zeus Thenatas at
Amnisos, and the torso of an Archaic kouros from Eleutherna.

On the other side of the room are cases (207) with hammered and
riveted bronze *Statuettes of the 7C B.C. from Dreros (a god, perhaps
Apollo Delphinios, for this was the name of the sanctuary, between two
other figures), and (208 & 209) the famous bronze shields from the
Idaian cave. These have lion's head bosses and repoussé decoration
showing battle and hunting scenes, an eagle gripping a sphinx, and the
Mistress of Animals. Other shields are from Palaikastro and Arkhades.
A bronze tympanon from the Idaian cave shows a god or hero
overthrowing wild animals to the beating of drums.

From Praisos comes a crouching clay lion, c. 600 B.C., in the centre of
the room. Behind the bronze statuettes are architectural members from
the 6C temple of Zeus at Palaikastro, showing running chariots and
dogs and Archaic relief pithoi. Against the wall on the right of the
entrance are lion's head water spouts from the Palaikastro temple, a
head from Axos (mid-6C), a Roman copy of the Archaic Hymn to Zeus
Cretagenes from Palaikastro, and a black stone stele from Dreros with a
winged human figure holding a bird.

GALLERY XX. CLASSICAL. HELLENISTIC, AND ROMAN SCULPTURES. Only the
most interesting or important pieces are listed here.
West Side (Left). Statues from Knossos. 273. Roman youth wearing *bulla* and
toga praetextata. 220. Portrait head of Homer. 315. Dionysus, with wreath of ivy.
46. Bacchus pouring from a wineskin (in alabaster). Doorway of Classical House
with part of the mouldings preserved. 5. Colossal statue of Hadrian with decorated
corselet showing the she-wolf suckling Romulus and Remus and two Victories
crowning Roma. 42. Torso of Aphrodite, probably a copy of a Praxitelean work.
8. (in front of Hadrian) Sarcophagus with inscription 'Polybos'. An orator
harangues the dead; below are the symbols of the Eleusinian mysteries.
North Side. Statues from Gortyn, mostly Roman copies of earlier works. 342.
Torso, copy of the Doryphoros of Polykleitos. 3. Good copy of winged Pothos
(Desire) by Skopas. The figure, wings missing, leans against a tree trunk. 325.
Aphrodite, copy of Alkamenes' (?) Aphrodite in the Gardens. 159. Torso of
Aphrodite, probably copy of a Praxitelean work. 43. Aphrodite kneeling in a bath,
copy of a work by Doidalsas. 347. Copy of the Athena Parthenos of Pheidias, the
cult statue of the Parthenon. 67, 65, 64, 66 1C A.D. busts of the family of Augustus,
Livia, Tiberius, Augustus, and Germanicus (?). 259, 260. Two Egyptian deities
identified with Persephone, and Pluto with Cerberus; from the Temple of Isis and

Serapis. 155. Fine head of Dionysus. 77. Head of Hera, copy of a Classical original. 326. Cult statue of Apollo Kitharoidos from the Temple of Pythian Apollo. 153. Pan playing the syrinx. 73. Over life-size head of the emperor Antoninus Pius (A.D. 131–61). 60. Bust of the emperor Septimius Severus (A.D. 193–211). 1. A bearded orator or philosopher with books at his feet, perhaps Herakleitos. 208. Artemis, indifferent copy of a Classical original. 350, 351. Hygieia, with the sacred snakes. 349. Aphrodite, copy of a Classical original.

East Side (Right). Statues from other Cretan Cities. 2. Female figure, probably Hestia, copy of a Classical original in the severe style, from Kissamos, W. Crete. 334. Roman empress, probably Julia Domna, wife of Septimius Severus and mother of Caracalla, from Chersonesos. 387. The Mallia Sarcophagus (3C A.D. ?). 265, 266. Two figures from the Death of the Children of Niobe at the hands of Apollo and Artemis, poor Roman copies, from Inatos. 74. Portrayal of a eunuch, from Lyttos. 317. Fine head of Trajan (A.D. 98–117), from Lyttos. 336. Good copy of a Praxitelean torso of Apollo or Hermes, unknown provenance. 230. Bust of Marcus Aurelius (A.D. 161–180), from Lyttos. 340. Bearded head, wearing a Persian helmet.

In front of the cult statue of Apollo is a mosaic floor, 2C A.D., from Knossos. It is by an artist named Apollinaris (see inscription) and shows Poseidon drawn by sea-horses, accompanied by tritons and dolphins.

South Side. Classical, Hellenistic, and Roman reliefs. 378. Funeral stele showing departure of dead man, imitating the 4C B.C. Attic type from Herakleion. 363. Metope, late 5C B.C., from Knossos. It shows a labour of Hercules, who brings the Erymanthian boar to the terrified King Eurystheus who takes refuge in a large jar. 249, 12, 10, 9. Fragments of Greco-Roman relief sarcophagi: the first, from Chersonesos, shows Atlanta's hunt of the Kalydonian boar and the others, from Gortyn, scenes of combat and Bellerophon and Pegasus. Other fragments from these cities show Eros and Tantalos. 145 Attic 4C B.C. funeral stele, showing a hunter, a notable piece, from the bay of Akhladha, Herakleion.

2   KNOSSOS

ROAD from Herakleion, 3¼ m. (5 km.); bus No. 2 from the Harbour viâ Plat. Elevtherias.—COACH EXCURSIONS daily in the late afternoon from Od. 25 Avgoustou.

We quit Herakleion by Plateia Elevtherias and beyond the walls turn S. just beyond (1 m.) the large cemetery church of Ayios Konstandinos an old paved Turkish road forking off left from the main road leads in c. ¾ m. to the site of the Royal Tomb at *Isopata* destroyed in 1942.—At 2 m. a road forks right for *Fortetsa*, the site of the Turkish encampment from which Herakleion was bombarded in the great siege. On the left is the site of the Medical Faculty of the University of Crete.

A hundred yards beyond the fork is a former Sanatorium (now a general hospital), in digging the foundations for which Late Minoan II warrior graves with rich finds (Herakleion Museum) were discovered in 1952. In the field above the main road opposite and beyond the Sanatorium was part of the Geometric cemetery of Knossos, while below the Sanatorium on the Knossos side are the remains of an early Christian basilica. In the right bank of the main road are the remains of the Roman *Amphitheatre* and a little farther on, in the field opposite, left of the road, of the *Roman Basilica*. Above the road on the right is (3 m.) the *Villa Dionysus*, a Roman building with fine mosaics of 2-3C A.D., depicting the Dionysiac cult. Just beyond this a short drive leads off right to the *Villa Ariadne* (formerly the house of Sir Arthur Evans and in 1926–52 the property of the British School at Àthens). It sheltered King Paul for a brief period after the evacuation of Greece, and was occupied by the German military commander during the occupation (comp. p. 64). It now has adjacent a stratigraphical museum (no adm.).

A hundred yards farther on steps lead up from the main road on the right to the Little Palace (see below).—3¼ m. *Knossos*. Large coach parks and all the paraphernalia of tourism mark the entrance to the site, but the village also has tavernas attracting an evening clientele.

KNOSSOS, the Minoan capital with its vast Palace and surrounding villas, dependent buildings and cemeteries, was excavated by Sir Arthur Evans and his assistant Dr Duncan Mackenzie from 1900, after 1951 (extensively in 1957–61) by M. S. F. Hood, and since 1967 by other members of the British School at Athens.

Admission 25 dr.; daily incl. Sun, summer 7.30-sunset; winter 9-sunset. The best detailed description of the site is J. D. S. Pendlebury's 'A Handbook to the Palace of Minos, Knossos' (London 1954). The Royal Villa, the Little Palace, and Royal Temple Tomb cannot normally be visited.

The reconstructions at Knossos, however controversial to professional archaeologists, give the ordinary visitor an immediate impression of the vast size and lavish conception of a Minoan palace-headquarters. To obtain more than an impression, a whole day's exploration is necessary. The text below notes the main points of interest, but visitors should be warned that owing to the many levels and the corridors that occasioned the myth of a 'labyrinth', it is not easy to follow a predetermined path without deviating. Those who wish to appreciate the ramifications of the building must wander at will with many retracings of steps. The central court is the best point of orientation.

Chronology of the site. *Knossos* was first inhabited at the beginning of the New Stone Age c. 6000 B.C. Gradually through the Neolithic period the mound of occupation debris accumulated here so that by the beginning of the Bronze Age, c. 3000 B.C., the Neolithic strata were up to 7 metres thick. Simple houses, roughly rectangular, were built, with walls, probably of mud brick, on a stone socle, and fixed hearths. Occupation continued through the Early Minoan period: of E.M.I date is a well, over 30 ft deep, in the N.E. Quarter of the Palace. Houses of E.M. II date were found on the S. edge of the Palace below the West Court and (1972–73) alongside the Royal Road N.W. of the Palace. E.M. III pottery has been recovered in recent excavations.

The first Palace seems, like that at Phaistos, to have been built late in or at the end of Middle Minoan IA, c. 1950–1900 B.C. Of this period, before the foundation, are extensive deposits of pottery below the earliest palace floors, notably the Vat Room deposit under the entrance leading N. out of the E. Pillar Crypt (Pl. 21), the Monolithic Pillars Basement deposit in the S.E. part of the Palace (Pl. 52), and under the West Court, where two houses of this period were excavated. The first Palace lasted from this foundation to the great earthquake destruction at the close of M.M. II, c. 1700 B.C. For the initial layout the earlier buildings on the top of the hill were erased and much of their material was dumped on the N.W. part of the site. From this unstratified pre-Palatial material have come fragments of imported pre-dynastic and early dynastic Egyptian stone vessels, important for demonstrating Minoan links with Egypt before the Palace was founded. There is evidence that at its beginning the first Palace consisted of a series of blocks, or *insulae*, the rounded corner of one of which can be seen on the N.W. corner of the Throne Room complex (Pl. 12). By the close of M.M. II there was considerable architectural unity: the great West Magazines had been constructed, as well as the N. Entrance Passage (Pl. 31), the Royal Pottery Stores and Magazines of the Giant Pithoi in the N.E. Quarter (Pl. 38) the complex on the E. side of the Central Court N. of the later East-West corridor (Pl. 41, 42), and a great cutting had been made on the E. side in which were rooms later remodelled into the Domestic Quarter. Tombs of this period and the next, M.M. III, lay on the slopes of Ailias hill opposite the Palace on the E., and others on the Acropolis hill to the West.

After the great earthquake destruction the Palace was rebuilt in M.M. III and it is the building of this period, with various modifications, which survives today. The main construction was in the Domestic Quarter with the building of the Grand Staircase, the Hall of the Double Axes, the Hall below it and the complex of rooms to the S. (Queen's Megaron). The N. Pillar Hall (Pl. 30) was built on to the remodelled N. Entrance Passage (Pl. 31). Modifications in the W. Magazines were made through the sinking of rectangular cists, or kasellas, into the floors of magazines 3-10 and in the Long Corridor beside them. Towards the close of M.M.

III, c 1600–1580 B.C., a severe earthquake necessitated some rebuilding and restoration of the W. Façade and S. Propylaeum (Pl. 3). At this time too the W. Porch (Pl. 1) was built and both the W. and Central Courts paved. In the W. Court this meant the covering of the great circular stone-lined rubbish pits (koulouras). Also in this period a new development took place, the building of a series of great houses around the Palace, the N.W. Treasure House and the House of the Frescoes, the S. House, House of the Chancel Screen and S.E. House being the main ones. Now also the Little Palace and a fine mansion behind it (excavated in 1967–72), the Royal Villa, and the Temple Tomb were constructed. These great dependent buildings correspond to the M.M. III-L.M. I villas and towns throughout the rest of Crete.

In Late Minoan I there were further slight modifications, including a good deal of fresco painting and in Late Minoan II the Throne Room complex as it now survives was built. The Palace was finally destroyed in a great conflagration c. 1400–1380 B.C. (This is the destruction date assigned by Evans and, though recently criticized, accepted by nearly all archaeologists, although there is disagreement about the nature and characterization of the period after c. 1400–1380.)

From the destruction debris of the Palace came large numbers of Linear B tablets. Most philologists have accepted the decipherment of this script as an early form of Greek. Knossos is the only place in Crete where Linear B tablets have been found, whereas Linear A, the Minoan language from which many of the Linear B signs were taken, is found at many places, notably the L.M. sites of Ayia Triadha and Zakro and on stone offering tables. Linear B tablets are of course well known from Pylos and Mycenae on the Mainland, in Late Helladic IIIB contexts, c. 1200 B.C. The presence of these tablets at Knossos together with a development in pottery decoration known as the Palace Style (Late Minoan II-IIIAi), a formalized and stylistic adaptation of the very naturalistic L.M. I vase painting and closely akin to mainland vase painting of this period, has led most archaeologists to accept that in its final phase, Late Minoan II-IIIAi, c. 1450–1400/1380 B.C., Knossos was inhabited by Mycenean Greek mainlanders.

After the destruction of the Palace there seems to have been some later reoccupation in Late Minoan IIIB, c. 1200 B.C., most notably in the Shrine of the Double Axes (Pl. 48) and in the Little Palace. After this date the Palace site was never again inhabited apart from a simple rectangular building, probably a Classical Greek temple lying between the staircase of the S. Propylaeum and the S.W. corner of the Central Court. Later ancient remains lie thick all over the Knossos region, but it seems that a tradition of sacred ground pervaded the Palace area, perhaps fostered by the idea of the Minotaur and labyrinth (perhaps from 'labrys' and meaning the House of the Double Axe), standard symbols of the coins of later Knossos.

A cemetery of L.M. IIIA date, contemporary for the most part with the final years of the Palace, lay at Zapher Papoura, the rising ground ½ m. due N. of the Palace. A richer and possibly royal cemetery of this time was situated at Katsamba, the harbour town of Knossos (see p. 76). Here a number of rich chamber tombs, reached by long dromoi, have produced L.M. II-IIIA vases in clay and stone and several Egyptian stone vessels. The Royal Tomb at Isopata, built in M.M. III, had its main burial in this period (see p. 52). Slightly later, L.M. IIIA-B, is a cemetery with 18 tombs recently excavated on Gypsadhes Hill, immediately S. of the Palace. There were a number of clay burial chests (larnakes) and the burial goods included a clay rhyton and stirrup vase and a bronze mirror, knives, and razor. Other L.M. III tombs have been found on the Ailias hill to the E. and elsewhere in the area. At *Sellopoulo*, c. 2 m. N.E. of Knossos, the L.M. IIIA tombs are contemporary with much of Zapher Papoura but much richer, as one recently dug has shown.

Later History. That there was a flourishing settlement in the Geometric period is shown by the contents of the cemetery to the N. of the site (comp. p. 52). Later Knossos became, with Gortyn and Kydonia (Khania), the leading city of Crete. Of 4C date are the remains of a temple recently traced on Gypsadhes Hill; here was found a large votive deposit of terracottas. In the 3C B.C., the city was a member of the Cretan Koinon, a loose federation of cities. After the war with Lyttos in 220 B.C., it lost the leadership of the island to Gortyn. During the 2C B.C., it was engaged in further conflict, first with Gortyn, then with Kydonia. It passed under Roman control after the conquest in 67 B.C., becoming in 36 B.C. a colony, Colonia Julia Nobilis, with veterans of Augustus. The Roman city was vast, stretching at least from the Vlychia stream W. of the main road (see Plan) to the area of the Villa

Dionysus, the amphitheatre and the basilica on the N. (see above). Strabo (10, IV, 7) gives the original circuit of the city as 30 stades (over 3¼ m). Though the 3C A.D. saw troubles and possibly a temporary break in life, habitation continued into the early Byzantine period, to which the 6C basilica S. of the Sanatorium and the adjacent early Christian cemetery bear witness. The bishop of Knossos was present at early Councils of the Church, in A.D. 431,451 and 787.

The ****Palace** is reached from the paved *West Court*. Note the large circular Middle Minoan rubbish pits below the court and at the bottom of one remains of Middle Minoan I houses, also the raised paved ways across the court and the altar bases in front of the *West Façade* of the Palace (see Plan). The well-cut limestone masonry in ashlar construction and the revetments of the walls, a characteristic feature of Minoan architecture, are very noticeable along the façade.

We enter by the *West Porch* with its column base preserved and inner room, perhaps for those awaiting entrance and for guards (Pl. 1). To the right of the porch are remains of later house constructions. The porch leads into the *Corridor of the Procession* (Pl. 2), so called because the walls were lined with frescoes depicting a procession of people bearing offerings. The Cup Bearer fresco (Herakleion Museum) is the best preserved of these figures, which resemble the Keftiu (Minoans) bearing their tribute on the walls of Eighteenth Dynasty Egyptian tombs. The Corridor originally went S. and turned l. to the *South Propylaeum* (Pl. 3). From the end of the Corridor as it is now we obtain a fine view of the southern dependencies of the Palace with the South House immediately below. To reach the Propylaeum now we turn left before the end of the Corridor. The Procession Fresco continued round to the Propylaeum and restored figures are now displayed on its wall. Also here are the large horns of consecration from the S. Front of the Palace. Immediately to the right of the monumental staircase was the small rectangular Greek temple, of which all traces have now been removed.

Ascending the staircase we come to the *Upper Propylaeum* (Upper Floor Pl. 4). This floor was restored by Sir Arthur Evans on the evidence of columns bases, door jambs, paving slabs, and steps which had fallen through on to the remains below. The walls of the lower story also helped to indicate where the upper walls stood. We pass to a tricolumnar hall (Pl. 5), off which was a small treasury (Pl. 6), filled with a great hoard of stone rhytons and other ritual vessels (Herakleion Museum). Thus the large hall may have been a shrine. From here the *Upper Long Corridor* (Pl. 7) runs N. with magazines (Pl. 8) and the halls opening off it on the left (Pl. 9). On the right it opens on to a series of rooms (above the Throne Room complex) in one of which (Pl. 10) are modern copies of some of the Palace frescoes. This room looks down on to the lustral basin beside the Throne Room. From the upper floor we may descend either to the *Central Court* by the monumental staircase with its column bases (Pl. 11; note at the top the marks of steps for an ascending staircase from the upper floor to a further story), or by a small private staircase (Pl. 12) to reach the Throne Room complex. The outer wall of this staircase at the bottom has its rounded corner dating from the First Palace.

The Throne Room is preceded by its *Antechamber* (Main Pl. 13) in which is a fine purple limestone basin, found in the passage immediately N. of this room. The **Throne Room** (Pl. 14) contains the gypsum throne with its guardian griffins (copies, originals in Herakleion Mus.) painted

Upper Floor
West Side

at same scale

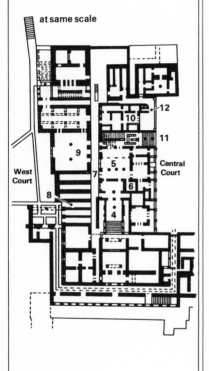

West Court

Central Court

12

10

11

9

7

5

6

8

4

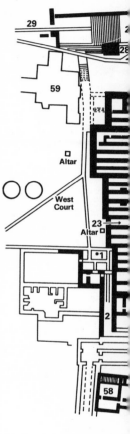

29

28

59

□ Altar

West Court

23

□ Altar

•1

2

58

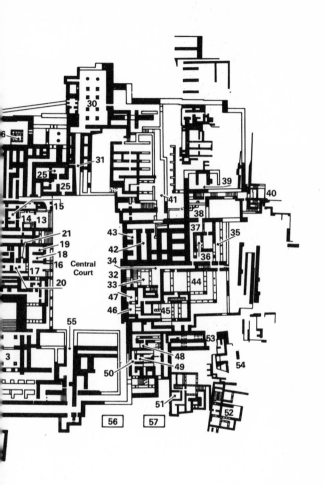

30

31

25

25

15

14 13

21

19

18

16

17

20

43

42

34

32

33

47

46

41

38

37

36

35

44

45

39

40

55

3

48

49

50

51

53

54

52

56

57

Central
Court

Palace of Knossos

0   50 metres

on each side. Benches line the walls, seats for those participating in ritual ceremonies, and opposite is the *Lustral Basin* entered by a descending staircase. Evans found dramatic evidence of the final moments of the Palace here in the Throne Room: overturned jars and the great flat gypsum alabastrons lying on the floor. Beyond the Throne Room was a small shrine which contained cult objects (Pl.15).

Coming out into the *Central Court* (58 yds by 29 yds) we turn right past the traces of a tripartite shrine (Pl. 16), like one portrayed on the Miniature Frescoes (Herakleion Museum), into the *Lobby of the Stone Seat* (Pl. 17), the *Room of the Tall Pithos* (Pl. 18) and the room beyond (Pl. 19) in the floor of which were two large Middle Minoan III cists, the Temple Repositories, containing the faience snake goddess, her votaries, faience flying fishes, and all the other furniture of a shrine. In the floor one of the later (L.M. I-II) cists is visible. From the Lobby of the Stone Seat the two *Pillar Crypts* are reached (Pl. 20). Note the double axe signs on the pillars and the channel at their base for liquid offerings. Under the entrance on the N. side of the first crypt was found the *Vat Room Deposit* (Pl. 21), of pre-Palatial, M.M. IА, date, c. 2000 B.C. From the crypts are reached the *Long Corridor* (Pl. 22) with the eighteen magazines opening off it (Pl. 23). Note the cists in the floors of some of these and the vast numbers of large clay pithoi, indicating the enormous storage capacity of the Palace. Marks of burning are clearly visible on the walls at the entrance to some of the magazines. In the corridor are several pyramidal stone stands for double axes on poles.

Proceeding to the top of the corridor and passing a narrow magazine where the Middle Minoan Hieroglyphic Deposit of clay sealings, labels, and bars was discovered (Pl. 24), we reach a complex of rooms (Pl. 25) in which the Saffron Gatherer and Miniature Frescoes were found. Below these are the M.M. I stone-lined pits, perhaps granaries or dungeons, as Evans thought. Beyond here is the N.W. Portico and N.W. *Lustral Basin* (Pl. 26), now restored. Outside and below this on the W. was found the alabaster lid with a cartouche of the Egyptian Hyksos king Khyan. From here can be seen the *Theatral Area* (Pl. 27) with its 'royal box' or loggia (Pl. 28).

The paved *Royal Road* (Pl. 29) leads out W. to the Little Palace. On the left of the road are Minoan houses, including the Late Minoan I HOUSE OF THE FRESCOES, and on the right was the ARSENAL, or Armoury. Beside the Armoury further excavations were made in 1957–61 and produced pottery deposits from Early Minoan II to Late Minoan III, as well as a fine series of ivories of L.M. IB, dating from c. 1500–1450 B.C. New excavations (1971–73) to the left of the road have revealed building remains from E. M. II (c. 2600 B.C.) to the 4C A.D. At the far end, on the left, a newly found road, precisely like the Royal Road in construction, leads off southwards. This and the Royal Road were built at the same time as the first Palace, c. 1950–1900 B.C.

Returning to the Palace we pass through the *North Pillar Hall* (Pl. 30) and up the *North Entrance Passage*, in which was found a large deposit of Linear B tablets, and flanking which is the great stucco relief (modern copy) of the charging bull (Pl. 31).

We now cross the Central Court to descend the *Grand Staircase* (Pl. 32), a masterpiece of Minoan architecture with its five flights of easy shallow steps, to the light well and *Hall of the Colonnades* at the bottom (Pl. 33). From here we continue along the lower *East–West Corridor*

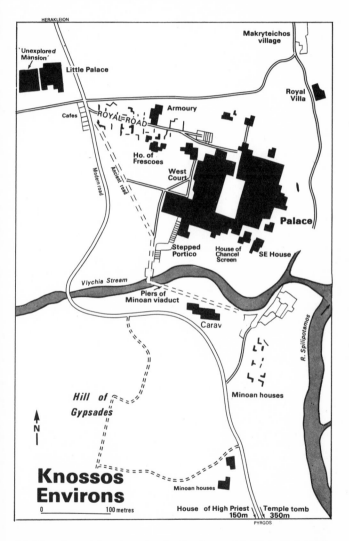

(Pl. 34) and turn left at the end to the *East Portico* (Pl. 35), behind which is a small storeroom with blocks of Spartan basalt (lapis Lacedaemonius) imported from the sole source, near Sparta, for making stone vases and gems (Pl. 36). Beyond these rooms are what may have been a potter's workshop (Pl. 37), the *Court of the Stone Spout* (Pl. 38) and *Magazines of the Giant Pithoi* (Pl. 39), mighty vases dating from the first Palace, M.M. II. Beyond these to the N. are the remains of the Royal Pottery Store also dating from M.M. II. A staircase descends from here to the *East Bastion* (Pl. 40). Walking down to the bastion, note the stone water channel descending a series of parabolic curves to break the flow of the water down the steep slopes. This shows a remarkable perception of hydrodynamics. Ascending the stairway past the Giant Pithoi we reach the *Corridor of the Draught-board* (Pl. 41) where the magnificent inlaid gaming board was found (Herakleion Museum). Below the corridor the clay pipes of the Palace's elaborate drainage system (or fresh-water system) are visible: notice how they taper (to produce a greater head of water to be driven through) and are carefully fitted together. From the corridor we pass the stone drain (which goes into the Court of the Stone Spout) to enter the magazine of the Medallion Pithoi, so-called from their decoration (Pl. 42). A similar pithos in stone was found in the Tomb of Klytemnestra at Mycenae. From here we return to the Grand Staircase along the *Corridor of the Bays* (Pl. 43), the thick walls of which must have supported spacious rooms above.

Before descending to visit the lower floor of the Domestic Quarter we may go along the Upper East-West Corridor past the Shield Fresco, into the restored *Upper Hall of the Double Axes*. Part of a Late Minoan II fresco with a bull's foot has been preserved here. Returning to the Grand Staircase we go to the bottom again. along the Lower East-West Corridor and turn into the *Hall of the Double Axes* (Pl. 44), a large reception hall divisible into smaller compartments and provided with columned porticos on the E. and S. From the S.W. corner of the hall we may pass to the *Queen's Megaron* (Pl. 45) with its Dolphin and L.M. II rosette frescoes. Below the floor part of the irregular paving of the first Palace floor is visible. Beside the megaron is the bathroom with clay tub provided. A corridor now leads us to the Queen's toilet with its remarkably modern fitments and drainage system (Pl. 46). Light is provided from the adjacent *Court of the Distaffs* (Pl. 47).

To the S. of this complex the S.E. rooms of the Palace can be seen. These include a bathroom (Pl. 48) and the tiny *Shrine of the Double Axes* (Pl. 49), of Late Minoan IIIB date, in which were found on a ledge at the back little idols with drum-shaped bases and little horns of consecration. On a pebble floor before these was a series of clay vases. The small corridor immediately W. of the shrine was called the *Corridor of the Sword Tablets*, since Linear B tablets of this class were found here (Pl. 50). Before leaving this part of the Palace we may visit the *House of the Chancel Screen* (Pl. 51), the *South East House* (Pl. 52), both M.M. III-L.M.I buildings, the M.M. IA Monolithic Pillar basement (Pl. 53) and a Minoan (L.M. I-II) kiln (Pl. 54).

We return to the Central Court in order to see the great Priest King (or Prince of the Lilies) fresco, set up in restoration on the wall below which the original fragments were found (Pl. 55). From here by passing along the Southern Corridor, which looks on to the remains of the *House of the Sacrificed Oxen* (Pl. 56) and the *House of the Fallen Blocks* (Pl. 57; named after the blocks of masonry that fell into it from the Palace), we can descend to another great building constructed after the earthquake in M.M. III, the *South House* or *House of the High Priest* (Pl. 58) with its several stories and pillar crypt remarkably well preserved.

The return is made by the Corridor of the Procession to the West Court, in the N.W. corner of which are the remains of the *North West Treasure House* (Pl. 59), so named because a rich hoard of bronze vessels was found there.

The *Stepped Portico*, the remains of the Minoan viaduct across the valley, and the *Caravanserai*, below the S. side of the Palace, all merit a visit.

The great dependent buildings are never open to the public, but can sometimes be seen by visiting specialists and are in part visible from outside the fences. To the S. of the Palace a small path leads down from the main road to the *Caravanserai* with its partridge and hoopoe fresco and adjacent Spring Chamber. This was the stopping-place for those coming from the S. before they went across the great viaduct, dating from Middle Minoan I, and up the ramp and stepped portico to the Palace. Proceeding S. along the main road, we find the *House of the High Priest* below the road on the left. It is designated thus because of its stone altar set behind a columnar balustrade, with stands for double axes on either side. Farther along the main road on the right is the **Royal Temple Tomb**, built in M.M. III but remaining in use until the destruction of the Palace. An open paved court leads to the *Inner Hall* and *Pillar Crypt*, beyond which is the *Sepulchral Chamber*. From the Inner Hall a small stairway leads to the upper floor which consisted of a two-columned room. The masonry of the lower rooms is excellently preserved and the whole building with its upper story recalls the Tomb of Minos in Sicily, built with its burial-place below and a temple above (Diodorus, IV, 79).

To the N.E. of the Palace lies the **Royal Villa**. The main hall, fronted by a portico with two columns, has a gypsum balustrade at its inner end and a throne set in the wall behind the balustrade. A fine purple stone lamp stood in the opening. To the N. of the megaron is a Pillar Crypt in which the slots in the masonry for the roof beams are visible. From here a stairway leads to the upper floor. To the S. of the megaron is another ascending staircase. On the landing of this was found a magnificent L.M. II Palace Style jar (Herakleion Museum) with papyrus in relief. The villa, like the other dependent buildings, was built in M.M. III.

Thirdly there is the **Little Palace**, just off the main road before Knossos is reached. This building, the largest explored at Knossos after the Palace, consists of a series of stately halls on the E. side, including a peristyle hall or court (comp. that at Phaistos). The E. façade seems to have had a columned portico. To the W. is a complex of smaller rooms and a staircase with two flights preserved. North of this is a Lustral Area, later, in L.M. III, used as a shrine with rough stones as images (the Fetish Shrine). In this late reoccupation the columned balustrade was walled up and this has preserved the impression of the convex flutings of the earlier columns. At the N. end of the building is a paved lavatory served by a drain behind running E.-W. The S. end of the Palace consists of a series of Pillar Crypts. That in the S.W. corner has a tiny walled recess on its N. side in which were found the famous Bull's Head rhyton, a double axe stand, and other religious objects. The Little Palace was built in M.M. III and destroyed at the same time as the main Palace. It contained at least one fine Palace Style amphora as well as Linear B tablets.

Since 1967 new excavations behind the Little Palace have revealed another large mansion with magnificent walls and a pillared hall of ashlar masonry. Scores of fine painted clay vases of L.M. II have been recovered from the destruction debris of this, the '**Unexplored Mansion**' of Evans.

3   EXCURSIONS FROM HERAKLEION

None of these excursions requires a whole day unless it be extended to the S. coast; either way the objectives are not suitable for an overnight stop. Though the first extends into territory that, strictly speaking, belongs in section II of the book, it is placed here for convenience.

A   To Tylissos, Anóyia, and the Idaian Cave

MINOR ROAD, asphalted, 20F m. (33 km.) to *Anóyia*, continuing viâ (26 m.) *Axos* to join the Rethymno road (Rte 11).—Tylissos (8¼ m.), which can be reached in ½ hr, makes a good separate early evening excursion.

We take the Khania road (Rte 11) and at 6½ m. (10½ km.) bear left through olive groves.—In (8½ m.) *Tíllissos* (ΤΥΛΙΣΟΣ), locally Tilissós, a picturesque village of 1170 inhab., the Minoan villas (open all day, fee) are signposted (l.).

TYLISSOS was inhabited in Early Minoan times, while in several places beside and under the later villas are traces of Middle Minoan constructions. The three large villas, of L.M. I date, are typical examples of fine Minoan country houses of this great age. They were destroyed about 1450 B.C. The finds in them were numerous and included many large clay storage jars, a fine bronze statuette of a man with a paunch, and pieces of miniature frescoes, one with boxers. The early, E.M.-M.M. I, buildings also produced quantities of pottery. Afterwards, as at Knossos and Ayia Triadha, there was considerable reoccupation of the site (L.M. III), including the building of a large circular cistern on the N.E. corner. There was also later Greek occupation and Tylissos at this time had its own coins.

House A, the central of the three houses, had its entrance on the E. (Pl. 1). Before it are traces of M.M. and L.M. III buildings. The northern part of the house contained two large magazines (Pl. 2) with a number of big storage jars, their bases set in the floor. The rectangular pillars in these rooms will have supported an upper story, reached by a staircase (Pl. 3) off the main hall. A paved corridor leads to the southern part of the house which contains other magazines (Pl. 4, 5), and a light well surrounded by three columns (Pl. 6). In one magazine (Pl. 5) were found the gigantic bronze cauldrons (Herakleion Museum) and some Linear A tablets. In the S.W. corner another staircase ascends to the upper floor.—House B lies to the W. It is smaller and less well preserved but below several of its rooms are walls of earlier buildings. In the N.E. corner was a staircase to the upper floor.

House C, like House A, is entered from the E. and there are also L.M. III walls at this point. In the eastern rooms a good deal of original paving survives. On the S. side a corridor leads from the paved vestibule to a staircase (Pl. 1). The rooms on the W. were magazines. In one of these (Pl. 2) is a column base dating from the rebuilding in L.M. III. The northern corridor (Pl. 3) has remains of the paving of this later period built over it. Off this corridor is a staircase of which the lower flight dates from the original L.M. I villa, the upper from a later Greek building. Opposite the corridor is a room with well preserved walls (Pl. 4); beyond is another room with a Greek block, probably a statue base (Pl. 5). To the N. of these rooms is a large hall with two columns (Pl. 6) having an open court on its W. side. To the N.E. of the house and built over its corner is a circular cistern of Late Minoan III date, entered by a staircase from the N. The water reached the cistern by a stone channel on the W. side, having first been decanted in a basin or trap at the W. end of this channel. Finally we may notice remains of a large early construction of E.M.-M.M. I date, N. of the house, among which is a Greek altar.

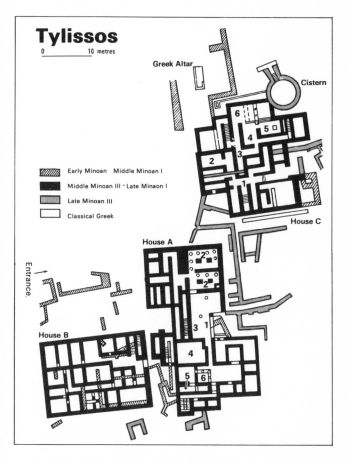

Tylissos

0   10 metres

Greek Altar

Cistern

6

5

4

2

3

House C

Early Minoan   Middle Minoan I

Middle Minoan III – Late Minoan I

Late Minoan III

Classical Greek

House A

2

Entrance.

3   1

House B

4

5   6

Beyond the village the road continues S.W. An abrupt hairpin bend starts a new climb with fine but brief views back to the coast. We pass through a rocky defile above a torrent into a long valley, at the head of which stands Gonies.—At 13 m., on the left side of the road, are the remains of the large Minoan villa of *Sklavokambos*. It is not as well built as the Tylissos houses and has walls of large, partly worked boulders. Of Late Minoan I date, it produced some clay sealings with impressions of fine gems, a stone rhyton and clay vases.—15¾ m. (25 km.) *Goniai*, with a prominent and very ugly church, stands on a hill of chloritic and serpentine rock. The road reaches a summit (2100 ft) at the nome boundary.

20½ m. **Anóyia** (ΑΝΩΓΕΙΑ), a mountain village of 2750 inhab., occupies a commanding position along a saddle (2390 ft). The place has a long tradition as a centre of resistance and revolt, for which reason it was burnt by the Turks in 1822, and by the Germans in 1944 for its part in sheltering the captors of Gen. Kreipe. It is noted for its weaving, many of the houses (rebuilt since the war) having their own looms.

From the village the ascent can be made in 4-6 hrs to the **Idaian Cave** above the upland plain of Nidha on Mt Ida (Psiloritis). There is also a very rough car track. The sacred cave (excavated by the Italian Mission) contained many rich finds of Iron Age date, 9C B.C., including the famous bronze shields depicting scenes of conflict in relief (Herakleion Museum). Descent to the S., see p. 67.

FROM ANÓYIA TO RETHYMNO, 53½ m. (86 km.) from Herakleion. The road drops steeply from Anóyia.—26 m. (42 km.) *Axós* is another high village with orange trees. Cretan dancing in the main square at night is now a weekly manifestation of tourist organization rather than an outburst of spontaneous local enthusiasm. Above the village (path signposted) on a steep acropolis, is the ancient city of the same name. There was a Late Minoan III settlement here but the city was fully established in the 8C B.C. (Geometric Period). Its walls survive in part and it has produced many relics, including its own coins and some bronzes.—The road decends on a ridge between two valleys to (31 m.) *Garázon* and (33 m.) the old Herakleion-Rethymno road (Rte 11).

B   Arkhanes, Vathypetro

ROAD, 11¾ m. (19 km.), asphalt to *Arkhanes*.

We take the Knossos road out of Herakleion and beyond Knossos pass (4½ m.) the fine Venetian aqueduct on two tiers of arches which brought water to Herakleion.—At 6¾ m. the road forks; this is the fateful T-junction where Patrick Leigh Fermor and W. Stanley Moss, with their Cretan band, kidnapped Gen. Kreipe in April 1944 while he was being driven from his H.Q. in Arkhanes to his residence in the Villa Ariadne. We branch right for (8 m.) *Káto Arkhánes* and (9¼ m.) *Epáno Arkhánes*.

Arkhánes (*Hotel Dias* **B**, S. of the village), as the latter is more simply known, is the leading grape-producing centre (3500 inhab.) of the island. Best known are its table grapes, rozakia (ροζάκια). In the village Sir Arthur Evans discovered a Minoan circular well-house. Recent excavations (I. Sakellarakis) near this (signposted above the Clock Tower) have revealed Minoan buildings contemporary with the last Palace at Knossos and built in the finest style of masonry. Minoan walls standing several feet high have been incorporated in some of the neighbouring houses. A water channel leads from the well-house and it may be that water was led to the Palace at Knossos from here. The church of *Ayia Triádha* in the village has early 14C frescoes, and that of the *Panayia* Byzantine icons.

Excavations in 1966–67 uncovered a Minoan cemetery on the hill of *Phourni* just N.W. of the village. The principal discoveries were an ossuary of c. 2500 B.C., and three well-preserved tholos tombs of c. 1400 B.C., one containing the first unplundered royal burial found in Crete. The sealed larnax held 140 pieces of golden jewellery of a Priestess-Queen, now displayed in Herakleion Museum. A splendid group of white marble idols of Cycladic type are among more recent finds. In 1971 at a short distance N. of Tholos A was uncovered a Mycenean-type grave circle. It comprised seven shaft graves, each of which contained an empty larnax, and had a bothros for a cult of worship. Bronze vases and stelai were found, but no bones, suggesting that the bodies had been deliberately exhumed at a later date in antiquity.

The church of the *Asomatos* (keys from guardian in Arkhánes village) lies c. 1 m. S. off the Vathypetro road to the left. It dates from 1315–16 and has early 14C frescoes, by Mikhail Patsidiotis, including a remarkable Crucifixion and a Capture of Jericho in which Joshua is depicted in Frankish armour.

From the village there is a rough road to the summit of *Mt Juktas* (2660 ft) on the W., now crowned by a radio transmitter, and affording a wide panorama of all this part of the island. On this summit a little N. of that with the church of Afendes Khristos, Evans discovered the remains of a Minoan peak sanctuary with a massive temenos wall, first built in M.M. I(?).

Beyond Arkhánes a rough road continues to (11¾ m.) **Vathypetro**, a Minoan villa, a short distance below the road on the right (signposted), overlooking the broad valley (*View to Kastelli). The *Villa*, of Late Minoan I date, is one of the largest known, and of particular interest in that remains of various industries and handicrafts are preserved, including a wine-press, oil-press, weaving rooms, and potters' workshops (the latter on the N. side). On the E. is a court with traces of a tripartite shrine of lighter construction than the villa walls. A long East-West corridor across the S. part, the well-built West façade with its cult niche, a main hall with three columns off the central court, and a great magazine for large storage jars on the S. side comprise other noteworthy parts of the building.

A poor road goes on from Vathypetro through *Khoudhétsi* (Rte 3C) to rejoin the main road which was left when forking off for Arkhánes.

C   The Pedhiadha

A pleasant day's round of c. 50 m. in a region with many frescoed village churches.

We leave Herakleion by the Knossos road and at the Arkhánes turn (Rte 3B) bear left to (9½ m.) *Kounávoi*. A short way beyond (11¼ m.) *Pezá* we bear left, and after another ½ m. left again.

The main S. road continues from Pezá viâ Khoudhétsi to *Khárakas* (20 m.) and *Pirgos* in the Anapodiáris valley, here separated from the Libyan Sea by the coastal Asteroúsia mountains.

The second branch to the right continues its picturesque way S.E. to *Arkalokhóri* (22¼ m. from Herakleion), a market village (2120 inhab.), near which in 1932 was explored a sacred cave used from Early Minoan I to Late Minoan times. It contained E.M. I vases with black pattern burnish, M.M.-L.M. I swords, and a series of small votive double axes in gold, silver, and bronze, many of those in gold bearing chased chased decoration and one or two with Linear A inscriptions. L.M. III tombs have since been found in the area.—From Arkalokhóri the road continues in the W. foothills of Mt Diktis to (40½ m.) *Ano Viánnos* (ancient *Biennos*), a large and picturesque village, on the highest part of which is the little church of Ayia Pelayia with interesting frescoes of 1360. About 3 m. before Viannos is reached, a road turns off right (S.) from the main road and in 2½ m. comes to *Khóndros*. About 10 min. walk from the village is an important Late Minoan III settlement, excavated by N. Platon. It covers a flat-topped hill called Kephala and has extensive remains of houses.

———

12¼ m. (20 km.) *Ayioi Paraskiaí* (850 inhab.). A pretty road runs eastward through (20 m.) *Apóstoloi* to (22½ m.) **Kastélli**, the chief village (1150 inhab.) of the Pedhiadha eparchy in the valley of the Karteros. Its Venetian castle survived until the early years of this century but is no more. Omar Pasha used it as headquarters in 1867. About ½ m. outside the village to the W. is a turning to the S. for *Sklaverokhóri*. Before entering the village (a few minutes only off the main road) we see on our left the late 15C church of *Eisódhia Theotókon*. It has well-preserved frescoes. Note especially St Francis on the N. wall; the Ancient of Days; a St George scene, approaching a castle with a princess and God's hand outstretched from above; a dramatic Transfiguration; and male and female river gods in the Baptism scene.

From Kastelli a by-road runs E. in 2 or 3 miles to *Xidás*, continuing above the village in a few minutes to the site of **Lyttos**, an important Classical city which minted its own coins. It was destroyed by Knossos in 220 B.C. Inhabited again in the Byzantine period, it had a large early-Christian basilica with mosaics which are in part preserved under the more recent church of *Ay. Yeoryios*. This has interesting frescoes with older marbles built in to the structure. Parts of the ancient walls and of a few buildings are still preserved on the terraced fields.

We return to Kastelli and turn N. to (25 m.) *Piyí*, a hamlet formerly known as *Bitzarianó*, Near by is Ay. Panteleimon, a large aisled basilica of late 12C or early 13C date. Recent work has revealed many frescoes: communion of the Apostles, Virgin holding the infant Christ (Vrefokratousa) in the coach of the apse, Virgin suckling the infant Christ, and Saints on the walls of the aisles. Much old masonry has been built into the walls (doubtless from ancient Lyttos) and the interior columns formed by piling as many as four ancient capitals one upon the other.

The road descends towards the N. coast, at 32½ m. joining the Lasithi road (Rte 6) and at 35¾ m. the coast road near Limín Khersonísou (Rte 5).

4 THE MESARA: GORTYN, PHAISTOS, AYIA TRIADHA

ROAD, 38 m. (61 km.), asphalt throughout.—28 m. (45 km.) **Gortyn.**—38 m. **Phaistos** and **Ayia Triadha.**—46½ m. *Ayia Galini.* Bus 8-10 times daily.

The road leaves Herakleion by the Pantokrator Gate, becomes Leof. 62 Martyron, and after 2 m. bears left for Phaistos.—3¾ m. By-road for *Ayios Miron* (11¼ m.), near which was ancient *Raukos,* an independent city which minted its own coins. The 13C Venetian church in the village has naves and aisles.—Our road runs moderately level through a gap in the hills, following the broad valley of Phinikiá, planted with olives and vines. The fields are carpeted in spring with wild flowers. At 10 m. we cross to the left (E.) side.—Between (11¼ m.) *Síva* and *Veneráton,* the next village, good retrospective view (r.) of Ay. Miron (comp. above), crowning a hill overlooking the next valley to the W.—13 m. (21 km.) *Avgenikí.* The road now winds up through olive groves to a less cultivated level, dominated on the right by a craggy outcrop surmounted by a chapel (the acropolis of Prinias, comp. below).—18 m. (29 km.) *Ayía Varvára* has a tiny church (Profitis Ilias) on a rock, said to mark the 'centre' of Crete. The area is subject to torrential rains.

In the village a by-road turns right for *Priniás* (3½ m.) near which on the acropolis, called Patela (2250 ft), is ancient *Ryzenia.* There are two Archaic temples, 7-6C, and, at the W. end of the hill, a square Hellenistic fortress with corner bastions. The temple sculptures (Herakleion Museum) include figures of a seated goddess and friezes of horses with their riders and lions.

To VALSAMONERO AND KAMARES. Near the end of the long village of Ay. Varvara a road to Kamares (asphalt to Zarós) turns right to run along the S. foothills of the Ida massif.—8¾ m. *Zarós,* a pleasant village with good water.—10½ m. Turning (r.) for the monastery of *Vrondísi* up on the hillside. The church has 14C frescoes. There is also a 16C Venetian fountain with worn statues of Adam and Eve. The church of **Valsamónero,** or Varsamonero, lies below the road, a little beyond the turning for Vrondisi. It may be reached by a path from (13¼ m.) *Vorizia,* the next village. The Italianate exterior of the church (Ay. Fanourios) is notable for its architectural details (14–15C). The 15C frescoes, ascribed to Konstandinos Rikos, are among the finest in Crete and include scenes from the life of the Virgin and a scene with John the Baptist in the desert. There is a fine wooden iconostasis. The Damaskinos icons in Ay. Aikaterini (Herakleion) came from Valsamonero.—At (15½ m.) *Kamáres* mules and guides may be hired for the 4 hr climb to the Kamares cave (4985 ft) on Mt Ida. This was the first place where the superlative Middle Minoan IB-II polychrome pottery was discovered and so gave it its name, Kamares Ware. The ascent to the summit of **Mt Ida** (Idhi Oros; 8058 ft), or *Psilorítis,* takes about 5 hrs from the cave. This should not be attempted without a guide. From the summit it is a further 4-5 hrs to the famous Idaian Cave, on the edge of the Nidha Plain to the N.E. (see p. 64). From this cave the descent to Vorizia takes c. 4 hours.

We cross (20 m.) the watershed and the whole **Mésara Plain** is revealed below. Its size, fertility, and favourable climate have ensured a concentrated agricultural population from Minoan times to the present day. The broad road winds down by hairpin bends (known as the Anegíri) through the foothills, with the temperature increasing at every turn.—27½ m. (44 km.) *Ayioi Dhéka* is named after ten martyrs of the persecution of Decius (A.D. 250). The aisled Byzantine church incorporates reused material from Gortyn. The stone is shown on which the holy ten are supposed to have knelt to be executed.

28 m. **GORTYN,** the capital of the Roman province of Crete and Cyrenaica, was the largest ancient city in the island. The main road goes through the middle of the city, our stopping-place being before the

basilica of Ayios Titos just off the road on the right.

The Acropolis, inhabited in Neolithic and again in Sub-Minoan times at the end of the Bronze Age, had a rectangular temple in the Geometric to Archaic periods (8-7C B.C.). Homer ('Iliad', II, 646) refers to this city as walled, though no walls survive today. The city in the plain below must have been flourishing by 500 B.C., for this is approximately the date of the famous Code of Laws (see below). In the Hellenistic period it was one of the group of allied cities in the Cretan League. Its harbours were at Matala and Lebena on the S. coast. In 220 B.C. it joined with Knossos against Lyttos; it is said to have received Hannibal in 189 B.C. After the Roman conquest (67 B.C.) Gortyn was made the capital of the province and it is from the imperial period, particularly the 2C A.D., that many of the great buildings date. The importance of the city was maintained in early Christian times, for it received Titus as first bishop, commissioned by St Paul to convert Crete. It continued as a religious centre in the early Byzantine period before the Saracen conquest c. A.D. 823–28.

Gortyn was excavated in the 1880s by the Italian Mission under F. Halbherr, and in 1954–61 by the Italian School, when the temple and altar on the acropolis were investigated. The whole area is littered with ploughed-out stones and pottery and systematic excavation has been undertaken in only a few places.

The basilica of *Ayios Titos*, 7C and later, has its apse preserved and traces of its early frescoes remain in one of the side chapels. Some of the original contents are in the Herakleion Historical Museum. Beyond the church we pass through the unexcavated Agora, a Greco-Roman market area, to the Roman *Odeum*, rebuilt by Trajan in A.D. 100. Into the back of this the Romans incorporated the Law Code of Gortyn. The code, inscribed, probably by 500 B.C., in a form of the Dorian dialect, is concerned with different classes of individuals and with civil and criminal offences including land tenure and inheritance, assault, adultery, and divorce. The 17,000 letters are written boustrophedon, i.e. one line from left to right, the next right to left and so on alternately. The Odeum was built on the site of earlier structures, including a 1C B.C. round building, itself made with material from an earlier round structure which originally bore the Archaic laws. A final restoration was effected in the 3-4C A.D.

Opposite the Odeum across the stream are the remains of a *Theatre*, built into the slope of the Acropolis hill. On the **Acropolis** is a rectangular *Temple* with its central bothros or circular pit (8-7C B.C.) on the site of the Late Minoan III—Sub-Minoan settlement. The temple contained a stone cult statue of three naked female figures (Herakleion Museum). Below the temple on the E. slope of the hill are remains of an altar of sacrifice, 14 yds long, near which was found a rich votive deposit with terracotta figurines, painted clay plaques with figures in relief and bronze objects of all periods from Late Minoan III to Roman. On the lower slopes of the hill on this E. side and across the stream on the opposite hill are remains of the aqueducts which brought water to the city from the region of Zarós (see p. 67).

We return to the main road to explore the remains on the S. side of it. These may be reached by a path from the main road about 500 yds back in the direction of Herakleion. The path, which is signposted, brings us first to the Temple of Isis and Serapis. Another path (see Plan) leads off E. from the Mitropolis road.

The Roman *Temple of Isis and Serapis* has a rectangular cella and annexes. The architrave records the construction of the building by Flavia Philyra and her two sons. Beyond is the apsidal **Temple of Pythian Apollo**, the main sanctuary of the city. It was built in the Archaic period on the site of a Minoan building of which there are traces of walls and gypsum paving inside the Hellenistic pronaos by the N. wall. The Archaic temple consisted of the rectangular cella and treasury at its N.E. corner. In the Hellenistic period the pronaos with six columns was added; four stelai between the intercolumniations were used to record treaties of Gortyn with other cities and with Eumenes II of Pergamon. In the 2C A.D. the apse and the internal Corinthian columns

of the cella were added. The altar before the temple and *Heroon* to the N. of the altar are Roman. A little distance S.W. of the temple are the remains of the brick-built Roman theatre and S.W. of this, across the E.-W. path, those of a Byzantine basilica church. To the E. of the temple (but also reached by another signposted path off the main road) is the *Praetorium*, the residence of the Roman governor of the Province. Like the rebuilt Odeum, this is of Trajanic date, extended in the 4C with a great paved basilican hall. Along the W. side are bases of statues of prominent citizens. The *Nymphaeum* was built towards the end of the 2C A.D. and transformed into a public fountain in Byzantine times. About 150 yds S.E. of the Praetorium are the remains of the *Amphitheatre* (2C A.D.) and about 200 yds S. of this are traces of the *Stadium*. To the W. of the amphitheatre is what survives of the *Great Gate*, a vast structure of Roman brick. Within are remains of the *Baths*.

A MUSEUM near Ay. Titos will display inscriptions and sculptures from the city. The building was finished but in 1979 not yet open. One inscription is of A. Larius Lepidus Sulpicianus, quaestor of Crete and one of Vespasian's commanders in the siege of Jerusalem in A.D. 70. Another inscription records Trajan's rebuilding of the Odeum. The sculptures include a head of Caracalla and a headless statue of Hermes-Anubis.

From Gortyn to Lebena, 17 m. (27 km.). From the main Herakleion-Phaistos road, a little before the Basilica of Ay. Titos is reached, a side road branches off for *Mitrópolis*, ¼ m. along, where some remains of an early Christian church may explain the name. Near here at *Kannia* is a Late Minoan I villa or farm with a shrine which contained clay figures of goddesses with raised arms. The road now crosses the Mesara plain to (3½ m.) *Plátanos*. About 150 yds W. of the village are remains of three tholos tombs, circular stone-built communal burial-chambers dating from Early Minoan to Middle Minoan I. There are many such throughout the Mesara but Tombs A and B at Platanos are the largest. From Tomb B came the significant Babylonian haematite cylinder seal of the period of Hammurabi. At Platanos we take the road left for (4¾ m.) *Plóra*, near which lay ancient Pyloros. We turn left on entering Plora and right a mile or so farther on (just before reaching Apesokári) to climb to (12 m.) *Miamoú*, and over the mountain to (17 m.) *Lénda* (ancient **Lebena**). The therapeutic springs made this a great sanctuary for healing. The temple of Asklepios (Asklepieion) dates from the 4C B.C. and the settlement flourished in Roman times, the temple being restored in the 2C A.D., the great building period at Gortyn, of which this was a harbour. The temple walls are of conglomerate blocks covered with brick and marble facings. The interior sides of the cella have mosaic pavements. The base for the cult statue of Asklepios by Xenion survives in the S.W. corner of the cella. Immediately N.E. of the temple is a Classical treasury which has fine mosaics of the Hellenistic period. Farther N. are porticoes separated by a marble staircase. Lying E. of the temple and S.E. of the E. end of the northern portico was the fountain built for the therapeutic springs. On the hill-side a little below the temple are two great basins, perhaps for the total immersion of the sick. The large building to the S.W. of the sanctuary complex is probably a hostel. Bounding the bay of Lebena on the W. is Cape Lion and N. of this is the Minoan settlement. S. Alexiou has excavated five Early—Middle Minoan tholos tombs near by. One lies E. at Zervou, two just W. of Lenda at Papoura, and two others c. 2 m. to the W. at Yerokambos. One of the last has produced a great deposit of vases of Early Minoan I date and from the whole group of tombs have come three Egyptian scarabs (Twelfth Dynasty).

From Lenda a fair but not asphalt road leads W. to *Kaloi Liménes*, the Fair Havens of St Paul (Acts, xxvii, 8). This is equated with the *Lasaia* of late antiquity and is connected with Míres by an asphalt road (14½ m).

At (33½ m.) *Míres* (Inn; 2900 inhab.) a colourful market is held each Saturday morning. Here a minor road left may be taken for Petro-kephalo and *Mátala* (10 m.), see below.—At 36½ m. a road turns left for the climb up to (38 m.) **PHAISTOS** (*Tourist Pavilion*, with R.). The bus stop and car park are just below the Tourist Pavilion, which is reached by a short paved path. The Palace has a superlative **Situation on a low, flat-topped hill, the easternmost of a chain which extends to Ayia Triadha; to the N. is the Ida massif, snowcapped for most of the year, while away to the E. stretches the Mesara plain, bounded on its S. side by the Asterousia mountains. More open, rolling country falls gently on the S.W. to the sea.

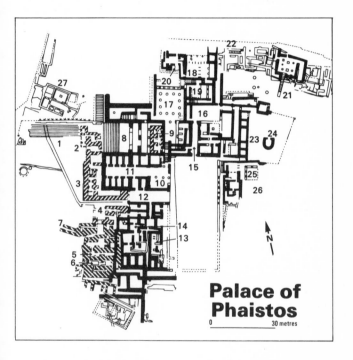

Palace of Phaistos

0 _____ 30 metres

The *Palace of Phaistos* and the surrounding area were excavated in 1900 and the following years for the Italian School of Archaeology at Athens, chiefly by L. Pernier. Since 1952 Doro Levi, Director of the Italian School, has made further extensive excavations on the W. side revealing many rooms of the First Palace. The site was inhabited in Neolithic and Early Minoan times since pottery deposits of these periods are found beneath the earliest Palace floors. The First Palace was built in Middle Minoan I. The excavations of D. Levi have revealed three distinct phases for this building before it was destroyed, like Knossos, c. 1700 B.C. Over this First Palace a thick cement-like fill was laid and upon this was built the Second Palace, which is mainly what is to be seen today. On the W. side the rooms of the first, M.M. I-II, Palace are preserved. The Second Palace was destroyed, like all the other major sites, c. 1450 B.C. in Late Minoan IB. There was some reoccupation in L.M. III at the end of the Bronze Age, and in the Geometric period (8C). Of the Classical-Hellenistic period are remains of a temple (first built in the 8C) and some fine houses. The city, mentioned in the Linear B tablets and by Homer ('Iliad', II, 648) was important in the later periods and minted its own coins, before it was destroyed by Gortyn.

The planning of the surviving ***Palace** is akin to that of Knossos and Mallia, the rooms being grouped round the large, paved central court (51 yds by 24), with a West Court across which ran raised paved ways. Certain areas had special purposes, religious and cult rooms being in the S.W. part, the Store-rooms N. of these, while the principal domestic apartments lay N. and, probably, E. of the Central Court. There is some evidence that the N.E. area contained workshops. Features distinctive to Phaistos are the tiered rows backing the Theatral area on the N., the monumental Grand Staircase, and the peristyle court. Also noticeable is that the W. façade of the Second Palace is set back from the rooms of the earlier building, making the Palace considerably smaller on this side, but giving it a larger West Court; this feature, therefore, remained common throughout the palaces' existence.

The visit begins in this **West Court** or *Theatral Area* (Pl. 1), where tiered rows provided seats for such events or ceremonies as took place here. In the N.E. corner at the foot of the Grand Staircase are a group of small rooms, a shrine complex of the First Palace (Pl. 2). In these were found a large clay offerings table, stone vases, and cult objects (Herakleion Museum). To the S. of these rooms and below the level of the court are the recently excavated rooms of the First Palace with their West Façade (Pl. 3).

The N. group of rooms (at present within a fenced area) was built (Phase I B, Middle Minoan IIA) after the S. group (Phase I A, Middle Minoan IB) and terminates in a corridor (Pl. 4) which provided a monumental entrance on the W. side. The S. rooms include a group of small magazines (Pl. 5) and a room with benches round the walls, perhaps a waiting room, entered by a staircase on the W. in the final state of the First Palace (Pl. 6). Attached to these S. rooms on the W. side is a ramp (Pl. 7). Overlying the same complex but set well back from it is the West Façade of the Second Palace.

To the W. of the wall bounding the Theatral Area, beyond a Minoan paved road, lies part of the town. Excavations since 1965 have brought to light more rooms of the First Palace period to the W. of those shown on the Plan and below the Tourist Pavilion. These (fenced off) belong to important houses that perished with the First Palace. From the whole complex has come an astonishing number of polychrome 'Kamares' vases, displayed in Herakleion Museum.

From the West Court the monumental *Grand Staircase* leads up to the *Propylaion* (Pl. 8). Below this are magazines of the First Palace which contained large clay pithoi with polychrome decoration (Pl. 9). From the Propylaion we descend by another staircase (r.) to the huge Central Court. Off this on the W. is an almost square pillared hall (Pl. 10). Beneath the floor and from the earlier Palace came an archive of clay sealings bearing seal-impressions of great variety. The hall leads directly to the double line of *Magazines* (Pl. 11), their heavy construction and the central pillars suggesting one if not more stories above. In one of the magazines on the right were gypsum slabs, dadoes, and variegated column bases fallen from above. To the S. of the magazines is a Corridor (Pl. 12) forming a monumental entrance on the W. side. Farther to the S. several of the rooms were for cult purposes: there is a pillar crypt (Pl. 13), as at Knossos, and a lustral basin (Pl. 14).

In the S.W. corner of the Palace at an oblique angle to its walls are scanty remains of a *Classical Temple*, founded in the 8C and perhaps dedicated to the Great Mother, Rhea.

From the Central Court a corridor (Pl. 15) leads N. to an internal court (Pl. 16). In the Central Court on each side of the entrance to this corridor are fresco decorations with a dark zigzag pattern on a light ground. A staircase from the N.W. corner of the Central Court ascends to a large peristyle hall (Pl. 17). From its N.E. corner a further staircase leads down to the northern apartments which are fenced off. They can all be well seen from the farther (E.) side. One was very possibly that of the king (Pl. 18), with door jambs indicating that it could be partitioned, and another of the queen (Pl. 19). A lustral basin (Pl. 20) stands adjacent to the king's room. This basin has been newly paved with gypsum slabs from near-by quarries at Ayia Triadha. On the N.E. edge of the hill lies a further complex of rooms reached by a staircase (Pl. 21). These are of First Palace date with much rebuilding in the Second Palace period. From one of them (Pl. 22), came the famous Phaistos Disk (Herakleion Museum). Returning to the Palace S. of this complex we pass workshops (Pl. 23) with an open court E. of them. In this court metal-working took place for there are remains of a large furnace in the middle (Pl. 24).

To the S. are further domestic apartments which produced fine Late Minoan I vases, an offerings table, and some bronze double axes. These rooms include a portico with columns on two sides (Pl. 25) and a hall divided by internal doors (Pl. 26). As we pass into the Central Court we may note the pillared façade (comp. Mallia).

Below the Tourist Pavilion and on the platform above the N. wall of the theatral area are remains of Hellenistic buildings, including an exedra (Pl. 27). On the S. slope of the hill Levi has excavated Middle and Late Minoan and Geometric (8C) to Hellenistic houses.

To Ayia Triadha. From Phaistos the motor road continues to Ayia Triadha (2 m.); alternatively on foot the pleasant path takes 45 minutes.

Ayía Triádha (named after the double-nave Venetian church 250 yds S.W. of the site) is beautifully situated just below the road end amid pomegranates and orange groves overlooking the plain and the sea. The place had some slight occupation in the Neolithic and Early Minoan periods. Middle Minoan I house remains were found under the Late Minoan I villa and town and a small group of rooms of this date is still visible (Pl. 18). The large villa (perhaps a small palace) and several houses are L.M. I (black on Plan). The site is notable for extensive L.M. III reoccupation after the destruction of the palaces and main sites in Crete (unshaded on Plan). In the Geometric period the central part of the large villa seems to have been a place of cult, for clay and bronze figurines of this date were found there. In Hellenistic and Roman times there was slight occupation. The church on the site, *Ay. Yeóryios Galatas*, is Venetian (1302) and has fresco remains. Notable are a rare scene in the apse of Christ lying down as a child, the Incarnation, and Redemption. The Minoan cemetery area lay to the N.E. of the site.

On entering the open, partly paved *Court* we see first, in the S.E. corner, a rectangular *Shrine* (Pl. 1), built in M.M. III-L.M. I, the floor of which was decorated with painted marine scenes (originals in Her. Mus.). The shrine was used in L.M. III and clay tubes with snake handles, like those from the Gournia shrine, were found in it. Beside the shrine are the remains of a large L.M. I *House* (Pl. 2) in which was found a fine bronze double axe with incised decoration.

The main rooms of the N. wing of the **Villa** or *Small Palace* consist, at the E. end, of residential or reception rooms (Pl. 3), W. of which are magazines with large clay pithoi (Pl. 4). Over these rooms were erected two large rectangular buildings on different axes from the L.M. I constructions (Pl. 5 and 6). Abutting the first of these later buildings and on the same axis is a kind of loggia (Pl. 7). Immediately W. of the main magazines is a small room with a channel for collecting liquids (Pl. 8). The residential apartments of the villa were in the W. wing. Here is a large hall with door jambs for partitions to divide it into smaller units (Pl. 9). A small chamber had a triple opening and benches round its walls, which were covered with a gypsum façade (now restored) with red stucco filling between the slabs (Pl. 10). This room leads on the left to a smaller chamber with a huge, slightly raised gypsum slab in its floor. Both rooms were lit by tall pedestal lamps (originals in Herakleion Museum).

From here we move to the archives room (Pl. 11), in which was found a deposit of clay sealings bearing impressions of numerous sealstones, and used to secure string-tied papyrus rolls and bundles. Next to this room is another (Pl. 12) the walls of which were covered with exquisite frescoes (Her. Mus.), including a seated lady in a garden and a cat stalking a pheasant. Immediately N. is a portico with a central bowl for rain-water (Pl. 13). On the stucco plaster of the walls were scored graffiti in the Linear A script. From one of the rooms to the S. of this complex (Pl. 14) came the famous serpentine relief cup with a band of soldiers and their captain. Bordering the W. wing and running N.-S. was a paved road (Pl. 15). From the main court we also see the small narrow treasury (Pl. 16) from which came the 19 bronze 'talents' or ox-hide ingots in Herakleion. In the court at the foot of a small stairway were found the fragments of the famous relief rhyton with boxing scenes (Pl. 17).

From the N.E. corner of the court a staircase descends to the '*Rampa del Mare*', a main way which runs along the N. side of the villa, leading W. towards the sea. On the N. side of this are traces of Middle Minoan *Houses* (Pl. 18) and farther on an L.M. III staircase adapted to the re-entrant façade of the villa (Pl. 19). Returning along the 'Rampa del Mare' we pass to a large L.M. I house, rebuilt in L.M. III, from which an L.M. III stairway descends to the **Town** area. Much of this is of L.M. III date, 14–13C B.C., a number of houses being built over or adapted from L.M. I buildings. On the right, opposite the town houses, is a row of magazines or shops fronted by a columned portico, an L.M. III building unique in Minoan architecture (Pl. 20).

. We leave this area at the N. end to visit the *Cemeteries*, a minute or so along the path to the N.E. Above the path are the remain of the two circular stone-built tholos tombs of Ayia Triadha, in use in E.M.-M.M. I. From them and the annexes outside them came many small clay and stone vases. Above the western of the two tombs was the Late Minoan cemetery area from which came the famous painted sarcophagus in Herakleion Museum. The tomb with four compartments like rooms cut out of the rock up on the hillside here produced an Egyptian seal of Queen Tyi (1411–1375 B.C.), wife of Amenhotep III, and a Hittite sphinx.

A little way along, through the olives, remains of Early Minoan buildings have recently been revealed. This may be part of the settlement of which the round tombs formed the cemeteries.

From Ayia Triadha an unpaved road descends to join the main Mesara road c. 1 m. S. of the Phaistos turn.

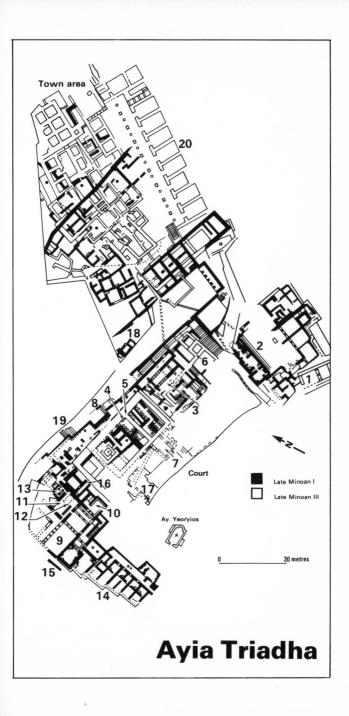

Town area

20

18

2

7

6

4 5
8
3

19

7

Court

13
11
16
12
10 17

9

15

14

Ay. Yeoryios

■ Late Minoan I
□ Late Minoan III

0 _____ 20 metres

N

Ayia Triadha

FROM PHAISTOS TO MATALA (7½ m.), good road, bus 5 times daily. From the car park the road continues S. and W.—4 m. *Pitsídhia* (Restaurants). At *Kommos*, 2½ m. S., excavations by the American School in 1976–77 suggested a large and prosperous town with occupation in MM II-LM III. Considerable structural remains have been uncovered from Classical times.—7 m. **Mátala** (*Matala Bay* C; good Restaurants), another harbour of Gortys, has ancient rock-cut tombs in the cliffs. There is good swimming.

Beyond the Phaistos turning the main Mesara road continues W. to (40 m.) *Timbáki* (3200 inhab.), a busy town with a street market (Fri). Beyond Timbáki the road climbs into low hills and crosses the nome boundary. At 44 m. a newly engineered road branches right towards Amári (comp. Rte 12A); our road bears left for Ayia Galini, joining the Spíli valley road on the approach to the coast.—46½ m. *Ayía Galíni*, see Rte 12B.

5   FROM HERAKLEION TO MALLIA AND AYIOS NIKOLAOS

NEW ROAD, 43 m. (70 km.); OLD ROAD (asphalt), 42¼ m. (68 km.), bus c. hourly (11 per day).—23 m. (37 km.) Palace of **Mallia**, N. of the main road (coach excursions).

The NEW ROAD, which most through travellers will take, duplicates the Old Road a little farther from the coast. The section by-passing Herakleion was not complete in 1979 and does not supersede the old road for the beaches or for visitors to Amnisos. In the area of Mallia its alinement is that of the old road. Farther on it keeps to the valley of the Gorge of Selenari, traversing a tunnel at the far end to avoid the pass, resulting in a shorter journey where some loss of scenery has to be balanced against a safer, smoother, and less arduous drive.

The old road (very busy on Sundays) leaves Herakleion below the Archaeological Museum and passes through the suburb of *Póros* where, on the right at *Katsamba*, a Neolithic house and a Minoan cemetery contemporary with the last years of the Palace of Knossos (c. 1450–1380 B.C.) have been excavated by S. Alexiou. At Poros in 1971 in an LM IIIв building was found a scarab of Ankhesenamun, wife of Tutankhamun. We pass in succession an Army Officers' Training School (r.), the Airport (l.), a small cave church, and a number of organized bathing beaches (NTO, Tobrouk, etc.).—At 4¼ m (7½ km.) a road branches right (for Episkopi) and in 1 m. reaches the **Cave of Eileithyia**, goddess of childbirth (below the road, on the left). The cave, mentioned by Homer ('Odyssey', XIX, 188), has stalactites (torch necessary) in connection with which the cult ritual took place. Pottery remains show that the cave was used from the beginning of the bronze age (E.M. I), if not from Neolithic, through to Roman times.

5 m. (8 km.) **Amnisos** (*Minoa Palace A; Xenia Karterou, Amnisos Beach* **B**, both W. of the site and closed in winter; the better beach lies to the E.). The low hill (*Palaiokhóra*) which rises from the sea-shore has Minoan remains at its base on each side (the ruins on the summit appear to be of a 16C Venetian village though on earlier foundations). On the W. are remains of substantial constructions (L.M. I), perhaps harbour works, for this was a port of Knossos; and on the E. the villa of the same date which produced the graceful frescoes of white Madonna lilies (Herakleion Museum). The Archiac Sanctuary of Zeus Thenatas, excavated by S. Marinatos, is at the foot of the hill near the shore on the

W. side. Hence Idomeneus is supposed to have sailed for the Trojan War. Farther W., on the site of the motel buildings, and below the shore line are the remains of the Late Minoan settlement. Amnisos, like Knossos, Phaistos, and Tylissos, is mentioned in the Linear B tablets.

The road continues along a coast where hotel development proceeds apace.—8 m. *Nirou Khani* (Arena, Knossos Beach **A**, just to the W.), conspicuous by its protective shelter (gate generally locked) at the landward side of the old road, is a fine large Minoan villa (L.M. I) with a paved front court. The rooms contained a store of religious furniture, including large, flat, bronze double axes and painted plaster altars.—9¼ m. *Goúrnes* (America **B**), where in the little valley to the right of the road Late Minoan III rock-cut tombs yielded jewellery, seals, and clay and bronze vessels. We pass a large base of the U.S Air Force. The old and new roads come together below a prominent hill, crowned by a large radar station, just before (12 m.) the turning (l.) to the *Candia Beach Hotel* (**A** with swimming pool).—14¼ m. (23 km.) Turning (r.) for Lasithi (see Rte 6).

16 m. (26 km.) *Limín Khersonísou* (Creta Maris **A**, to the W.; Nora **B**, to the E.; Belevedere **A**, higher up inland; Rest. Rodanthi, by the road, good), a rapidly growing community of 785 inhab., makes tiles and is expanding untidily into a flourishing holiday resort with a caravan camping site. The ancient city of **Chersonesos** (see below) extends from the village westwards for a considerable distance, but to the layman offers little of interest. It was the harbour town of Lyttos (comp. p. 66) but was independent and minted its own coins, through which its ancient name is known. It seems to have been founded in the 5C B.C., had a famous temple of Britomartis-Artemis, mentioned by Strabo, and achieved its greatest importance as the seat of a bishop in early Byzantine times.

A road (l.) in the village soon passes (l.) a much restored pyramidal Roman fountain decorated with spirited mosaics showing expeditions to catch various kinds of fish. A concrete path leads to the church of Ayia Paraskevi on the promontory. From the E. side of the point, when the sea is calm, the Roman quays may be seen with their stone bollards, slightly submerged in the bay below; this demonstrates the rise in sea level here since ancient times. On the summit of the promontory hill are the remains of an early Christian basilican church (6C) with curvilinear mosaics. The form of the apse is well preserved; it is unusual, being included in a rectangle. Below the church at the N. point of the promontory, rectangular Roman fish tanks are cut in the rock at sea level. Vestiges of the theatre survive. The remains of another basilica church with mosaics are preserved on the edge of the sea c. ½ m. E. of Khersonesos village.

18¾ m. *Stalís* (Anthousa Beach **A**; Blue Sea **B**). A bad track climbs inland to Mochós and Lasithi.—20 m. Ikaros Village (Bungalow Hotel **A**), with a flourishing souvenir pottery industry.—21 m. (34 km.) *Mállia* is a large village, pleasanter than is suggested by its brash highway façade, from which a road leads through wind-pumps and banana groves to the fine sandy shore (Grammatikakis **C**, good) where new holiday hotels (Kernos Beach, Sirens Beach **A**, Mallia Beach **B**, etc) are conspicuous.—At 23 m. we turn left from the main road for the Palace. The site called **Mallia** lies in the coastal plain at the foot of the hill, crowned by the little chapel of Ayios Ilias, that forms the seaward spur of *Seléna* (5114 ft). The ancient name of the place is not known.

The **Palace of Mallia** and the surrounding villas and cemeteries, have been systematically excavated by the French School of Archaeology since 1922 after the Greek archaeologist, J. Hatzidhakis, had discovered it and made some preliminary investigations. Mallia is somewhat larger in area than Phaistos though poorer architecturally.

The site is described in detail in 'Guide des fouilles françaises en Crète' (1966), published by the French School.

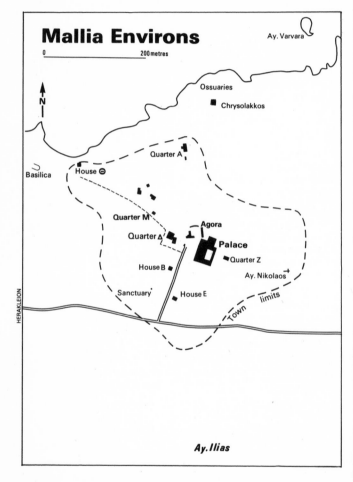

The Palace, like those of Knossos and Phaistos, was founded in Middle Minoan I. c. 1900 B.C., and suffered a great destruction contemporary with that of the other palaces, c. 1700 B.C. The rebuilt Second Palace lasted until Late Minoan IB, c. 1450 B.C., when it was destroyed, like the surrounding houses and the other major sites of the island. A few parts of the Mallia site, notably House E, were reoccupied in L.M. III. after the Palatial Age, while one building within the Palace (Pl. 12) appears to be later because its walls have a different alinement. The surviving remains of the Palace and Houses are almost entirely those of the Second Palace period, M.M. III-L.M. I.—In its general plan, with rooms, magazines, staircases, and corridors disposed round the rectangular central court, Mallia resembles the other great Palaces, but it has a number of individual features.

The Palace is approached from the *West Court* with its paved ways; one of these serves the North Entrance (see below), another runs parallel with the W. front. At the S. end, and contemporary with the First Palace, is a group of eight circular structures, each c. 17 ft across, which

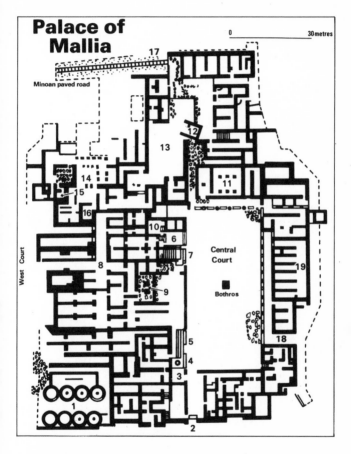

Palace of Mallia

0   30 metres

17

Minoan paved road

12

13

14

15

11

16

10

6

7

Central Court

8

19

9

Bothros

West Court

5

4

18

3

1

2

were used as granaries (Pl. 1). We follow the S. front just inside the fence, passing the narrow opening to a shrine, to the main *Entrance* (Pl. 2), a flagged passage between walls. This was probably cut off from the main court by an extension of the wall at the end, so that entry was made by turning left through a door into an antechamber (Pl. 3), which gave on to a paved terrace (Pl. 4) opening directly by two steps on to the central court. Here, set in the floor, a circular stone table (kernos) has 34 small depressions round a large central one; its function seems more likely to have been secular than religious. Just to the N. is a Monumental Staircase (Pl. 5).

The CENTRAL COURT, more than twice as long as it is wide (52 yds by 24), had a different elevation on each side, and each wing differs greatly in plan. In the exact centre is a *Bothros*, or shallow pit.

To the E.of the Cental Court are the E. entrance corridor (Pl. 18) and the *Magazines* (Pl. 19) behind the portico of alternating circular and rectangular columns (comp, the portico on the E. side of the Central Court at Phaistos). The magazines (now within a locked shed) have raised benches for vessels and channels for collecting liquid. Oil and wine were presumably stored here.

Off the Central Court to the W. are what seem to be cult or official rooms, inculding a raised platform (Pl. 6), perhaps for ceremonial purposes, and a *Grand Staircase* (Pl. 7). Between this and the more southerly stair (comp. above), and served by many doors from a Corridor (Pl. 8) running down the W. side, are a number of interconnecting rooms including a flagged *Pillar Crypt* (Pl. 9) like that at Knossos opening from a large hall. Cult symbols are carved on the pillars. From the W. corridor we may return through storage rooms with huge pithoi to the raised platform (comp. above) and its associated suite of rooms. Of these the 'Hall of the Leopard' (Pl. 10) yielded to the excavators an axe-head in the shape of a leopard, and a sword, both in Herakleion Museum (gallery IV).

The N. Wing was fronted by a colonnade, the bases for which remain *in situ*. Behind extends a large *Hall* (Pl. 11) with 6 rectangular pillars to support a suite, presumably of large rooms, on the upper floor. Part of a staircase remains to the E. and another exists farther N.

We follow a corridor which is partly obstructed by a later building (Pl. 12) on an oblique alinement. This faces the North Court (Pl. 13) and its orientation has been shown to correspond with certain exceptional appearances of the full moon above Mt Seléna.

Farther W. open the principal apartments of the palace, including the *Megaron* (Pl. 14) with its antechamber and a *Lustral Basin* (Pl. 15) and the palace *Archives* (Pl 16), which yielded tablets in hieroglyphic script as well as in Linear A. To the N. extended the garden of the Second Palace which covered the foundations of the First Palace (Middle Minoan I). We return to the North Court in order to leave the palace by its *North Entrance* (Pl. 17). A fine paved way still leads up to the gateway; near by stand two huge pithoi.

Around the Palace and of the same period as its surviving remains are a series of large houses, part of a town of considerable size which remains to be explored. Immediately to the N. lies the *Agora*, subject of recent excavations. To the W. of the Palace and N. of the Excavation House is the so-called *Hypostyle Crypt* (conspicuous by its protective cover) below ground level and approached by a staircase. The building consists of a series of stores and two interconnected halls with benches round three sides. The purpose of the building may have been to provide a place for refreshment and deliberation of the city fathers.

Behind the Excavation House to the W. is 'Area Δ' (kept covered) another series of houses with a paved road between them. In the centre of one house is a lustral basin or bath having walls of white plaster with a red dado.

In Area M. to the W. of Area Δ, a large building of First Palace date has been excavated. Here in 1968 came to light a further hieroglyphic archive deposit. The building, possible a palace, has the earliest sunken lustral basin yet known in Minoan architecture.

Farther W. (nearly ½ m.) from the Palace, at *Marmara*, are the ruins of an Early Christian basilica (6-7C), built over a tomb which contained a sarcophagus of the Antonine period (2C A.D., possibly in re-use), now in Herakleion Museum. North of the Palace towards the sea are the cemeteries. Before these is found the large *House A*, built at the time of the First Palace, Middle Minoan I. Beyond this, 500 yds N. of the Palace is *Khrysolakkos* (Pit of Gold), a large rectangular burial enclosure with several compartments, contemporary with the First Palace. It may have been a royal burial-place for it is elaborately built and from it came the famous gold pendant of two conjoined bees (in Herakleion). It has been suggested that the famous Aegina treasure in the British Museum was actually plundered from here during the latter part of the 19C. The presence of clay idols indicates that some of the rooms on the E. side were for cult purposes. To the N. of Khrysolakkos on the rocky bluff are natural caves which were used as ossuaries during M.M.I, while in the bay of the Ay. Varvara islet to the E. are further remains, including workshops, dating from the period of the First Palace.

To the E. of the Palace (and reached from its E. entrance by a paved way) is Area Z. Here three houses have been excavated; that to the left of the paved road shows the best construction. Note its paved hall with column base at the entrance and door jambs for a series of openings within.

Two further excavated areas may be visited on the way back to the main road. On the E. side of the Palace approach road is the large **House E**, of M.M. III-L.M. I date, but reoccupied after the Palatial Age. Off the W. side of the approach road remains of another building have been found. It has Horns of Consecration incorporated in its construction and may therefore have been a shrine.

The old and the new roads merge for a while. Continuing eastwards we suddenly enter the *Gorge of Selenári*, where the cuttings for the new road have left unsightly gashes. The holy ikon of St George of Selenári has, however, been given a new and more sumptuous setting above the junction of the old and new roads where bus passengers can still dismount to pay their homage. The new road now keeps lower with only occasional access to the Neapolis or Elounda roads and avoids the pass by a tunnel. The old road remains narrow and awkward.—28½ m. *Vrakhásion* stands near the head of the pass. Beyond the summit (1310 ft) the views are spectacular towards the S.E. *Latsidha* stands on the old road to the E. of the new.—33 m. (53 km.) **Neápolis** (*Neapolis* **D**), a market town (3100 inhab.) and the seat of the eparchy of Mirabello, has a large plateia shaded by Mediterranean pine, round which are grouped the bus station, town hall, and post office. There is a small *Museum* (key from the Gymnasion) with antiquities from the Minoan cemetery at Elounda (comp. below), several sealstones and a clay potter's wheel with a Linear A inscription. There are also finds from the archaic city of Dreros. In the antecedent village of *Kares* in 1340 was born Petros Philargis, or Philagros, who became Pope Alexander V in 1409–10 during the schism.

Dreros is reached by leaving Neapolis on the Ay. Nikolaos road, turning left at *Nikithianó* (1¼ m.) for *Kastélli* (3¾ m.; asphalt). Here a minor road leads left and the site lies a short distance farther on the hill Ayios Antonios. Remains preserved on the hill with two peaks separated by a saddle include walls on the E. and W., houses on the slopes, supported by retaining walls, the Archaic *Agora*, to the S. of which is a Geometric temple, the *Delphinion*, consecrated to Apollo Delphinios, and a large cistern of the Hellenistic period. From the Delphinion came important Archaic statuettes of hammered bronze (Herakleion Museum). A much ruined building, S. of the Delphinion, is evidently the *Prytaneion*, the public hall for the magistrates and for the reception of official visitors. The cemetery lay to the N. of the eastern of the two summits. The ancient name is known by an inscription found in 1855 but removed to Constantinople.— From Kastelli this road continues to Elounda (see below), then down the coast to Ayios Nikolaos.

Farther on an asphalted loop road to the right (followed by the bus) serves the village of *Khoumeriákos*. The tedious descent through scrubby hills is avoided by the new highway. We join the road from Lasithi (Rte 6) and leave (l.) a direct road (by-passing Ayios Nikolaos) to Elounda.

42¼ m. (68 km.) **Ayios Nikólaos**, see Rte 7. The main highway by-passes the town, continuing towards Siteia (Rte 8, 9).

6   THE LASITHI PLAIN AND THE CAVE OF ZEUS

ROAD, 37½ m. (59 km.) to *Tzermiádhon*, continuing to (44½ m.) *Psikhró* for the cave.

The excursion to Lasithi is much recommended, both for the dramatic climb to the top of the pass which cuts through the girdle of mountains round the Lasithi plain, for the plain itself with its thousands of wind pumps, and for the Dictaean Cave, a traditional birthplace of Zeus, near Psykhro. Intending visitors to the cave should take rope- or rubber-soled shoes, an old pair of trousers, and a sweater.

From Herakleion by the Ayios Nikolaos road to (14¼ m.) the Lasithi turn, see Rte 5. We turn inland and at 18 m. leave on our right the road for Kastélli Pedhiádha (Rte 3c). Keeping left in the Langádha valley we skirt (21 m.) *Potamiés*, where the church of the Panayia Gouverniótissa has frescoes of the 14C (Christ Pantokrator in the cupola) and 15C.— 24¼ m. *Avdhoú*, producing olive oil, has been a centre of Cretan revolts. In the village the church of Ay. Antonios has faded 14C frescoes exposing the finely-drawn original sketches. Note SS Peter and Paul exchanging a kiss. About ½ m. W. of the village is a cemetery church. Ay. Yeoryios, also painted (14–15C). Ayios Konstandinos, a little S.W., has Last Judgement scenes, painted by Manuel and John Phokadhas (1445–46). We start to climb, completing three sides of a rectangle round *Goniés* to make height. A by-road runs N. to *Mokhós* (2 m.), a large village (1500 inhab.) whose main square is the scene of an animated festival on 15 August.

28¾ m. (46 km.) *Krási* (2035 ft), ½ m. left of the main road on an asphalt loop, has a copious supply of spring water below vaulted draw-basins, and an enormous plane-tree which twelve men cannot girdle. Near by is an Early Minoan circular stone-built tholos tomb discovered by Evans and excavated by S. Marinatos in 1929.—30 m. *Kerá*, just below which, by the road, is the monastery of the *Kardiótissa* (12C), with frescoes. The monastery contained a famous ikon of the Virgin, taken to Rome in 1498.

The road now climbs steeply to the Selí Ambélou pass (2950 ft; café), the lowest part of an almost continuous ridge, marked by a remarkable row of derelict stone windmills. There are splendid retrospective *Views down the gorge to the sea and forward towards Diktys. Beyond and below lies the upland **Plain of Lasithi** (Oropédio Lasithíou), filled with countless wind-pumps; each has 4–8 triangular sails of white cloth which revolve anti-clockwise to draw water to the surface. The stream which irrigates the plain is drained off by a swallow-hole at its western end. The irrigation works were designed by Paduan engineers during the Venetian occupation (c. 1463). The plain, too high for olive cultivation, but fertile in apples, potatoes, and other vegetables, and growing also barley, is encircled by dominating mountains: Selena to the N. Aphendes to the W., Katharo and Varsami to the E., all about 5000 ft, while to the S. rises Spathi (7050 ft). It has been inhabited since Neolithic times, though it was virtually deserted in the Classical and Hellenistic era.

37½ m. (59 km.) *Tzermiádhon* (1130 inhab.; Inn) is the principal village of the eparchy. To the N. and reached in ¾ hr on foot, the summit of *Karphí* held a Minoan refuge city dating from the very end of the Bronze Age (c. 1100 B.C.). The town of **Karphi** was excavated by the British School under John Pendlebury in 1937–39 and the buildings are well-preserved. One's bona fides should be established with the phylax since it is suspected that undug areas are subject to local looting.

Whether the approach is made from the W. end of Tzermiadhon by track, upland plain, and scree slope; from the Seli Ambeliou pass along the crest; or (most steeply) from Kerá, Karphi is not easy to find.

The site was occupied in the 'sub-Minoan' period by refugees who built in a fashion reminiscent of the mainland but worshipped Cretan gods: the excavators suggested a brigand-city of diehards (some 3500 strong). It must have been desolate, windy, and snowswept in winter and was eventually abandoned without violence. The principal remains include a *Temple* (from which came some of the large clay goddesses with raised arms in Herakleion Museum, gallery XI); the *Tower* and so-called 'Barracks' (not a certain identification) guarding one steep entrance; the *Great House*, probably that of the chief or king; and a characteristic 'Homeric' house of the simplest type.

The associated tholos tombs near a spring below the town suggested to the excavator an Achaean ruling class; no more normal Minoan style burials have come to light.

In the hills immediately E. of the village are the *Cave of Trapeza*, with remains from Neolithic to Middle Minoan I; and the site of *Kastellos*, a Middle Minoan settlement.

After Tzermiádhon the road turns S. and soon divides at a modern church. The left branch, for Neápolis and Ayios Nikólaos, is described below.—The right branch (signposted 'Moni Kristalenias') follows the E. verge of the plain through Ayios Konstandinos.—41 m. *Ayios Yeóryios* has a modest hotel and there is a Byzantine site on the rocky knoll a short way off in the centre of the plain. We bear left for (44½ m.) *Psikhró*.

At the end of the village, a turning (l.; signposted 'Spileon') leads up to

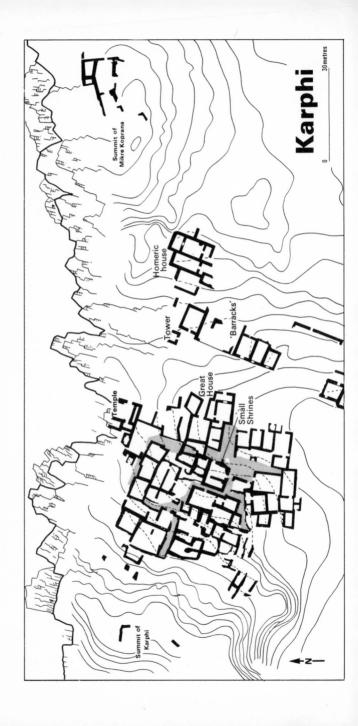

Karphi

Summit of Mikre Koprana

Homeric house

Tower

'Barracks'

Temple

Great House

Small Shrines

Summit of Karphi

N

0   30 metres

a Tourist Pavilion, from which a stepped path ascends (15 min.) to the *Cave of Psychro* (guides available at Tourist Pavilion; small fee per person in a group; or bargain). This may be the *Diktaean Cave* where the Hymn of the Kouretes says Zeus was born. An oracle had decreed that Kronos would be dethroned by his son, so his mother Rhea, to protect the child from his father, gave him to the Kouretes to conceal in the cave. That Kronos might not hear Zeus' cries, the Kouretes beat their shields. The cave, excavated by D. G. Hogarth (B.S.A. 1899–1900), produced remains from Middle Minoan to Archaic Greek times. Notable are stone tables of offering, one (in Oxford) inscribed with Linear A signs, and a series of small bronzes. Near the top of the steps we pay an entrance fee (the ticket-boy provides water for washing hands on the way down and deserves a tip). The descent into the cave is steep and somewhat slippery, and the lower depths are chilly. The upper part of the cave contained remains of a temenos, or sacred enclosure, with an altar; to the S. is the entrance to the main cavern, which descends 210 feet. There are fine stalactites. Water lies in this lower part for most of the year.

The summit of *Mt. Diktys* (7045 ft), to the S., affords an unsurpassed **View over the entire island. Excursions are made in summer (apply at the Tourist Pavilion; sleeping-bag necessary), starting at 5 p.m. on the arranged evening. One hour's mule ride brings to a deserted small church where the night is spent. Before first light the ascent is continued (1 hr more by mule; 2-3 hrs on foot) to the summit. On the leisurely descent a great variety of bird life, butterflies, and flowers (comp. B.S.A., v. 38, p. 147) can be seen.

FROM TZERMIÁDHON TO AYIOS NIKOLAOS, 27½ m. (44 km.). At the road junction (comp. above) we bear left on an asphalt road. After a further mile, in *Mésa Lasíthi*, we bear right and climb out of the plain by the pass of *Patéra ta Seliá* (3600 ft) and descend to *Mésa Potámos* (Restaurant) in a valley of holm-oaks below the summit of Selína. After a second col, with a cluster of derelict stone windmills, we descend the long valley enclosed between Makhairá (4877 ft) to the N. and Katharón Tsíthi (5457 ft) to the S.—12 m. *Zénia* has a prominent quarry. After a sharp descent the road forks l. for Neapolis, right for Ayios Nikolaos.— At 17½ m. we join the old Neapolis–Ayios Nikolaos road, passing under the new highway (no access).—27¼ m. **Ayios Nikolaos,** see Rte 7.

7   AYIOS NIKOLAOS AND ITS ENVIRONS

AYIOS NIKOLAOS, a little harbour town (5000 inhab.), pleasantly situated on the W. side of the Gulf of Mirabello, has developed without losing its charm into the fashionable resort of Crete. It has the unusual distinction of being the chief town of the nome (Lasithi) but not of the eparchy (Mirabello) in which it is situated. The Gulf of Mirabello is known to air travellers of the 30s as the half-way stop for Imperial Airways' flying-boats between Phaleron Bay and Alexandria; here in 1936 the 'Scipio' crashed with the loss of two passengers, though crew and five others were rescued and all the air mail salvaged.

Approaches. Road from Herakleion, see Rte 6; from Ierapetra and Siteia, see Rtes 8, 9. By sea, see p. 16.
Hotels. On the coast N. of the town: **Minos Beach,** 120 bungalows, DPO, L, open all year; **Mirabello,** 175 R, air conditioned, **A** (also 130 bungalows **L**), both these with private beach, swimming pool, tennis, etc.

In the town: **Hermes** (Pl. a), 200 **R**, swimming pool, **A**: **Coral** (Pl. b), 135 R, DPO, **B; Creta** (Pl. g), small and good; **Akratos** (Pl. d), **Alcestis** (Pl. e), **Du Lac** (Pl. f), **Rhea** (Pl. c), 110 R, **Delta** (Pl. h), these all **C**. and others.

Youth Hostel (60 beds), 3 Stratigou Koraka.

Restaurants. *Cretan* (Vassilis); *Charis*, on the harbour; also on the shore at N. end of Akti Koundourou.—Cafés round the harbour and by the lakeside.

Bookshops. *Rafaelakis*, 46 Leof. Koundourou, and others higher up.

Bus Station, see plan. Services to *Herakleion* (11 times daily); to *Ierapetra* (6 times); to *Kritsá* (10 times); to *Siteia* (5 times); to *Elounda* (frequently).

Steamers to Siteia, Karpathos, and Rhodes.

Coach Excursions (with guide) by Knossos Travel, once or twice weekly in mid-March–mid-Nov, to most places in E. Crete.—Caique or launch excursions to Elounda, Spinalonga, etc., Tues, Thurs, & Sat aft; to Pseira and Mokhlos, Fri morning.

Anciently *Lato pros Kamara*, the harbour of Lato (p. 88), the place has never been of major importance. The Genoese built a castle in the 13C which was abandoned in the 17C, and the growth of a modern town dates only from 1867.

The short LEOFOROS KOUNDOUROU, attractively tree-lined, descends from the main square to the harbour. To the left a small channel, dug in 1867–71 and crossed by a bridge, links the harbour with a small circular lake, 210 ft in depth. On its landward side a steep cliff is provided with an aviary, from which the harsh cry of peacocks echoes over the swimming club's racing lanes.

The broad esplanade running N. from the bridge provides a pleasant stroll by the sea. Here the Hermes Hotel (1973) is architecturally interesting, particularly for its interior design.

On the road leaving for Herakleion from the harbour office stands the **Museum** (closed in 1979 for an indefinite period). Eight rooms round a central court are arranged chronologically clockwise. ROOM 1. Pottery from Myrtos and Mokhlos.—R. 2 (l.) Finds from burial enclosures A and B at Zakro; finds from Mirsini, with good Late Minoan pottery, are continued in Room 3. Here also are objects from Kritsa tombs; jewellery, including necklaces, and seals from Sklavi and from sites in the Siteia area; Mycenean larnakes with painted fish from Papoura.— ROOM 4. Sub-Minoan to Geometric pottery from Khamaizi, Praisos, Siteia; figurines.—R. 5. Archaic goddesses and figurines from Olous; note the tortoises and wild pigs.—ROOM 6 contents unknown.—R. 7 contains various later finds from the Siteia region, including three carved gemstones; contents of a Roman tomb from Ayios Nikolaos.—ROOM 8. Local folklore.

Motor boats (excursions, see above) may be hired for visits to the islands of Pseira and Mokhlos, both having Late Minoan I settlements; Mokhlos (dug by the American School in 1908) also has Early Minoan stone-built tombs (from which came the exquisite stone vases and gold diadems in Herakleion Museum). Permission may sometimes be granted to visit *Ayii Pandis*, an island reserved to the kri-kri, which breed here.

FROM AYIOS NIKOLAOS TO ELOUNDA, 7½ m. (12 km.), asphalt road. At (2 m.) *Sta Lenika* are remains of a 2C B.C. temple dedicated to Aphrodite and Ares and excavated by the French School in 1937. After crossing a headland the road drops down towards the modern village of *Elounda* (Astir Palace, 200R, Elounda Beach, 300 R, DPO, L; Aristea **C**). Before the village, where the road reaches sea level, tracks lead (r.) to salt pans (largely disused). Dating from the Venetian period, these were fed latterly by a canal cut through the isthmus of Poros which joins the Spinalonga peninsula to the mainland. A causeway and bridge lead to a restored mill. The unexcavated site of Ancient **Olous**, the port of Dreros, is strewn with pottery, and near the canal ancient walls can be seen below the surface of the sea. In a field to the N.W. of a small church is an excavated *Basilica* with lively fish mosaics, almost the only remains visible above ground of a city that had temples of Zeus Talaios and Britomartis. It was often in conflict with Lato (see below),

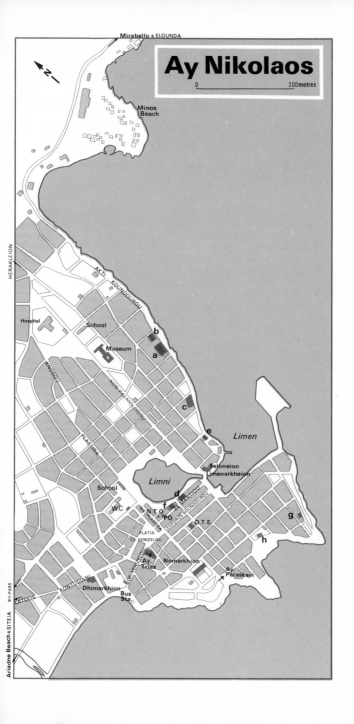

especially in the 2C B.C. Towards 200 B.C. it concluded a treaty with Rhodes. The stone walls surrounding the carob orchards are doubtless witness to much destruction by plough. A Late Minoan III cemetery lay at *Stous Traphous* on the mainland immediately S. of Olous. At the N. end of Spinalonga the Venetians built a fortress in 1579 (see the inscription of the Provveditore over the Main Gate on the W. side) and separated it from the isle by cutting a channel. It thus controlled the large natural harbour between Spinalonga and the mainland. The Turks did not gain the fortress till as late as 1715. After they left in 1904 it became a leper colony but is now uninhabited. Inside the melancholy *Fortress Venetian and Turkish buildings may be seen, including vaulted cisterns on the W. side. The name Spinalonga, probably a Venetian misinterpretation of 'stin Elounda', survives an absurd official attempt in 1954 to change it to Kalydon.

From Elounda the asphalt road continues to Fourni and Dreros (see above) and then joins the main Herakleion road.

FROM AYIOS NIKOLAOS TO KRITSA (7 m.; asphalt) AND LATO. We leave the town as if for Siteia, cross the new highway, and continue S. through an area quarried for gravel. The road levels out amid olive groves with Mt. Diktys ahead.—5¼ m. The *Church of the Panayia Kéra*, to the right of the road, is usually considered the finest church with fresco paintings in Crete and dates from the early years of the Venetian occupation. The S. aisle has scenes from the life of St Anne, the Virgin's mother, St Joachim, and the infant Mary, the N. aisle scenes from Paradise, while the central paintings are devoted to the life of Christ, the Last Judgement and the punishment of the damned. On the sanctuary ceiling, Ascension. Other frescoed churches in the district should be seen, especially Ay. Georgios Kavousiotis (14C) on the S.E. edge of the village to the left of the road to Kroustas. Near Kroustas are two more.

At the village of (7 m.) *Kritsá* is the motorable track (3 m. farther; c. 1 hr on foot) for ancient Lato, now known as *Goulás*. We keep to the right at two forks to reach the site which, as usual, covers two acropolis peaks and the saddle between. *Lato was founded in the Archaic period (7C B.C.) and is of interest for its early town plan, but is principally to be enjoyed for the beauty of the situation which makes it one of the most striking ancient places in Crete.

Though securely identified by an inscription during the French School's exploration of 1899–1900, *Lato* lay largely ignored in favour of Minoan sites until excavations were begun again in 1967. A thorough exploration involves much clambering, but the central area (Pl. inset) is easily accessible. The road now ends somewhat above the ancient entrance and may occasion missing the most striking approach.

An imposing *Gate* with two inner doorways gives on to a square court from which a long stepped street rises at right angles. This is bordered on the right by shops and workshops which open from the steps and back on to the defensive wall itself. On the left are a defensive tower and several narrow doorways leading into the N. sector of the town. The street bends right and then left to reach the AGORA, a small pentagonal area with a sanctuary and a reservoir in the middle. A stoa bounds the W. side and an Exedra the S.W. On the N. between two towers a triple flight of steps gives access to an upper terrace on which stood two altars. The arrangement suggests the Minoan 'theatral area' that is so characteristic a feature at Knossos and Phaistos. The towers form part of a secondary fortification wall but it is not at all clear how this functioned in relation to the other.—Higher up to the N.E. is an edifice thought to be the Hellenistic *Prytaneion*.

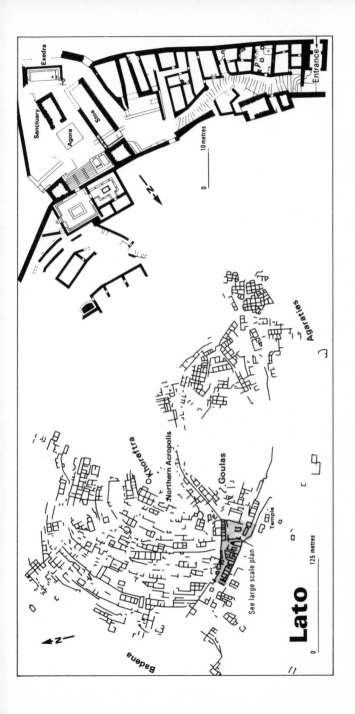

Lato

Sanctuary

Exedra

Stoa

Agora

Entrance

N

0   10 metres

Khoréttra

Northern Acropolis

Badéna

Goulas

Temple

See large scale plan

Agaráties

N

0   125 metres

Above the S.E. corner of the Agora, on a terrace supported by a rustic polygonal retaining wall, well preserved, stand four courses of a *Temple*, rectangular with pronaos and cella, comparable with the Aphrodision at Delos and to be dated near the end of the 4C. B.C.

8   AYIOS NIKOLAOS TO IERAPETRA (AND MYRTOS)

ROAD, 23¼ m. (37 km.), asphalt. 12¼ m. (19 km.) **Gourniá**.—23¼ m. **Ierápetra**. Bus 6 times daily.

From the town an approach road soon joins the N. coastal highway. We turn left and follow the *GULF OF MIRABELLO* amid outstanding scenery.—3 m. *The Cretan Village* is an attractive group of villas for holiday hire.—Near (8 m.) *Kaló Khorió* is **Vrokastro**, a site excavated by the University of Pennsylvania in 1910–12. It is approached by an arduous climb (no path) from near the model farm on the highway. Though remains go back over the previous thousand years, most important are those of the Geometric level, consisting of a village of poor houses built of rubble masonry.

12 m. **Gourniá**, the most completely preserved Minoan *Town, was excavated in 1901–04 by the American archaeologist, Harriet Boyd Hawes. It was founded in Early Minoan times but most of the surviving remains are L.M. I, with one or two houses reoccupied in Late Minoan III. The phylax has studied the flowers (superb in early spring) as well as the history of the site. Features to be noticed are the narrow streets and connecting stairways, a Middle Minoan I house on the N.E. corner of the site (Pl. 1), the Palace (Pl. 2), or residence of the local ruler, with its magazines (Pl. 3) reached by a staircase from the open court (Pl. 4), houses of the Reoccupation Period (L.M. III, 14-13C B.C., Pl. 5), and a little shrine (Pl. 6) in which were found clay tubes with snakes modelled in relief, an offerings table and a clay goddess with raised arms. Among the best preserved houses are those of the Carpenter (7), where sets of saws were found, of the Potter (8), and of the Smith (9). Near the entrance is a room where remains of an oil-press were identified. On the shore are remains of Minoan houses, associated with the port (now submerged). The best general idea of the ruins is obtained from the hillside across the road to the N. of the site. A rocky mule path shortens the walking distance to Pakhyammos.

13¾ m. *Pakhyammos*, officially Pakhía Ammos (Golden Beach C), a growing place with small hotels, stands at the parting of the ways to Siteia and Ierapetra. Here a Middle Minoan cemetery with burials in clay jars (pithoi) was excavated on the beach by the American archaeologist R. B. Seager.

We turn S. across the narrowest part of the island in a broad valley affording the lowest crossing between the N. and S. coasts. To the left is the massive Thripte range with a dramatic gorge opening into the mountain. Off the road to the right lies *Vasilikí* with its important Early Minoan II settlement (2600–2300 B.C.). Note the holes for timbers in the red-plastered walls. The buildings produced many beautiful clay vases with mottled decoration and the site gives its name to this Vasilike ware.—Beyond the sizable contiguous villages of (17¾ m.) *Episkopí* and *Káto Khorío*, the plain is irrigated by wind-pumps.

23¼ m. **Ierápetra** (ΙΕΡΑΠΕΤΡΑ; *Kreta* **C**, and others more modest) is the only large town (6600 inhab.) on the S. coast of Crete and a favoured summer resort. The *Museum* (next to the Dhimarkhion, closed in 1979) has the finest Minoan clay larnax in the island, from near-by Episkopi.

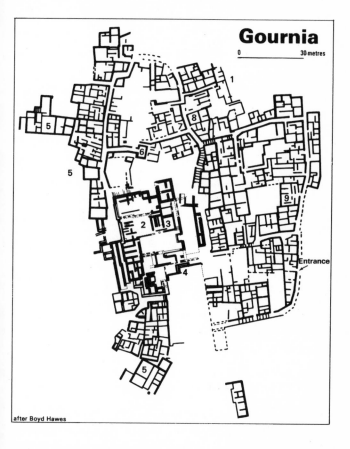

It is of Late Minoan III date and is painted with amusing hunting scenes. There are also antiquities from the Roman city, *Hieraptyna*. This lies just outside the modern town on both sides of the coastal road to Viannos. On the seaward side traces of the theatre survive. The city made a treaty with Rhodes in 201 B.C. but did not reach its acme until Roman times. The fortress was built by the Genoese on a small promontory at the beginning of the 13C. The near-by minaret and Turkish fountain are worth seeing and a house near these is said without much evidence to have been occupied by Napoleon on his way to Egypt on the night of 26 June 1798.

FROM IERAPETRA TO MYRTOS AND VIANNOS. A new road (part of the projected S. coast highway) runs W. At 8¾ m. on the steep-sided hill of Fournou Korifi (r.) is the Early Minoan settlement of of **Myrtos**, called after the modern village which lies 2 m. farther on. This was excavated by the British School (Peter Warren) in 1967–68, when c. 90 rooms were uncovered. These represent two periods of urban occupation of E.M. II date, c. 2500 and c. 2170 B.C. Many evidences were found of the manufacture of pottery and textiles, and a room on the S.W. corner of the site proves to be the oldest known Minoan domestic shrine. The clay goddess figurine and some of the 700 clay vases with othet objects of daily life are displayed in Ayios Nikolaos museum. A subsidiary collection is at present on show in the Myrtos village school.

About ½ m. farther on, immediately before the river-bed E. of Mytros is reached, a high hill called Pírgos stands above the road to the right. A site here, now called **Pyrgos**, was excavated by the British School (Gerald Cadogan) in 1970–75. This proved to be a Minoan settlement of long duration, dominated in the Middle Minoan III-Late Minoan I period by a large country house which faced across a court to the sea. In its second phase, possibly a rebuilding after an earthquake, it was given a S. façade in ashlar and a fine staircase to an upper floor. Notable are the floors of variegated stones, especially the porphyry common in the area. One Linear A tablet was recovered. The house was burned down in Late Minoan IB.

The new road climbs inland above the village of *Myrtos* by many twists and turns over the S. slopes of Diktys. The terrain is rugged with some fine scenery.—Near (20 m.) *Káto Sími* a sanctuary of Hermes and Aphrodite has been excavated. A building (MM IIIB/LM IA) with seven rooms and a paved court apparently gave place to an open-air sanctuary of which a Protogeometric altar has been found.—Beyond *Pefkos*, at 24½ m. a steep and unmade road branches left through Amirás skirting a fine gorge to *Arví* (9 m.; Ariadne C), a village on the coast with a rebuilt monastery and tavernas.—27 m. *Viánnos,* see Rte 3C. The main road continues W. to Skhiniás and is planned to go through to the Mesara.

9   AYIOS NIKOLAOS TO SITEIA AND ZAKRO

ROAD, 72 m. (115 km.). Broad highway to (43¼ m.) **Siteia**, asphalt to (54¼ m.) **Palaikastro** and (narrower) to (67 m.) *Ano Zákro*; rough but in course of improvement for the last few miles. BUSES to Siteia (p. 86); change for Palaikastro (infrequently).

To (13¾ m.) *Pakhiammos* passing **Gourniá**, see Rte 8. We pass inland of a hill whose W. face falls sheer to the sea.—17¼ m. *Kavoúsi,* planted with pink and white oleanders. The road climbs on the eroded slope of Kapsás above the offshore islet of *Pseira*. The *View is especially fine in the opposite direction in the evening when the sun sets over the mountains behind Ayios Nikolaos (pleasant café at Platanos). The cliffs above Mokhlos are white with gypsum. High above the coast, the road turns inland through the foothills of Ornón, passing a series of verdant villages.—At (27¼ m.) *Sfáka* is a turning left for Mokhlos village (4½ m.) from which Mokhlos island can be reached by boat in a few minutes. *Tourlóti* stands on a promontory to the left of the road.—At (30¼ m.) *Mirsíni* the church has good Venetian doorways. Near here, on the slopes of Aspropilia hill, an Early to Middle Minoan tholos tomb and Late Minoan III rock-cut chamber tombs have been excavated by N. Platon.

The road crosses a high spur to (34 m.) *Mésa Moulianá* near which, at *Selládhes*, were found L.M. III tombs with swords and fibulae dating from the very end of the Bronze Age; and *Exo Moulianá*, noted for its red wine. A col marked by ruined windmills affords the first sight ahead of the Siteia plain.—At (38½ m.) *Khamaízi* a prehistoric house, oval in plan, was excavated in 1904. The site lies on a hill just S. of the road before entering the village. A new investigation by K. Davaras in 1971 clarified the plan and distinguished several phases of use in E.M. III-M.M. I (2200–1700 B.C.). *Skopí* lies below the main road to the right as we descend into the plain.

43¼ m. (73 km.) **Siteía** (ΣΗΤΕΙΑ; *Siteian Beach* A; *Siteia, Alice, Crystal*, all C; etc; Y.H.; boat connections for Karpathos and Rhodes), seat of an eparchy and of the Bp. of Hierapytna and Siteia, a friendly town of 6200 inhab., has a pleasant frontage, tree-lined and with several good restaurants. The little port exports raisins. Above the port the Kastro has few old buildings save the restored Venetian fort at the top. The town is identified with the ancient *Eteia* of Stephanus of Byzantium, though no ancient site is preserved. Myson, one of the Seven Sages of Greece, is said to be from here, as also was Vincenzo Kornaros, author of the 17C Cretan literary epic, the Erotokritos. *Sitia* (formerly La Sitia, hence Lasithi) was walled and given a fortress by the Venetians but suffered from earthquakes in 1303 and 1508 and at the hands of Barbarossa, the Turkish pirate, in 1539. The English traveller Bernand Randolph records the Turkish pasha selling wheat for export here in 1680.

The Minoan villas near Piskokéfalo and Praisós, described in Rte 10, make an interesting excursion from Siteia.

The road now runs E. round the bay, which is being developed and landscaped. The flat-topped hill ahead has the appearance of a fortress. Many natural outcrops of ˙rock in the area could be mistaken for cyclopean walls, but the countryside is neither impressive nor beautiful. At *Ayía Fotiá* a huge Early Minoan cemetery with more than 250 tombs was excavated by K. Davaras in 1971.

We turn inland. At 52¼ m. a bad road forks left for the isolated monastery of **Tóploú**, or *Panayia Akrotiriani* (1¼ m. on foot; by car it is better approached by way of Vai, comp. below). The monastery, founded in 1365 (though there was an earlier church), was called Our Lady of the Cape in Venetian times and Toplou ('cannon-ball') from the Turkish period. It has a long tradition of hospitality to refugees and wayfarers and as a resistance centre. In addition to its architecture it has several objects of interest, a Hellenistic inscription (c. 138–132 B.C.) found at Itanos and describing the relations of Itanos and Hierapytna with Magnesia in Asia Minor, one of the earliest editions of Suidas (10C A.D.), and several fine ikons including the famous 'Lord, Thou Art

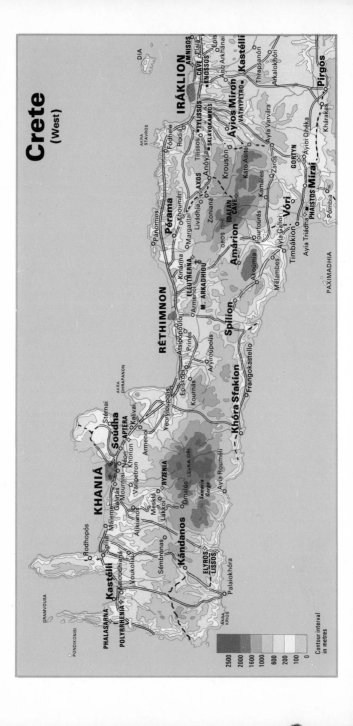

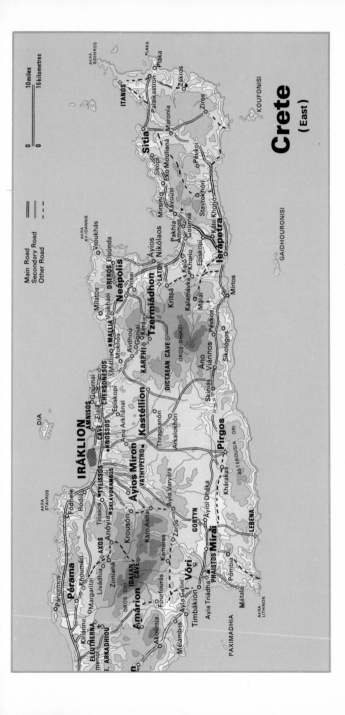

Crete
(East)

Great', painted by Ioannes Kornaros in 1770, one of the great masterpieces of Cretan art.

54½ m. (88 km.) **Palaíkastro** (*Itanos*, small) stands near the base of Cape Plaka. The Minoan town lies about 20 min. E. of the village through the olives towards the sea. Take the path to the sea from the village and walk over open ground to the right after emerging from the olives. The site was occupied from early in the Bronze Age (Early Minoan II) but the preserved remains are, as at Gournia, Late Minoan I. A typical house, excavated by the British School in 1962–63, lies to the right of the main street. On the E. part of the site remains of a temple of Dictaean Zeus were found. The prominent hill *Kastri*, N. of the town, was occupied in Early Minoan times and then again at the end of the Bronze Age (Late Minoan III C). To the S. a Middle Minoan I peak-sanctuary with many human clay figurines and several stone libation tablets with Linear A inscriptions was found on Mt Petsofa.

FROM PALAIKASTRO TO ITANOS. A new road runs to (2¼ m.) *Vái*, where a remarkable grove of tall palm trees (despite the local legends about Arabs, probably *phoenix Theophrasti Greuter*, a wild date-palm indigenous to Crete) fringes a fine sandy beach (taverna). The road continues to (4 m.) *Erimoúpolis* (Itanos **C**) at the base of Cape Sidheros. Here ancient **Itanos** (r.) occupied the usual double acropolis; the plan is best understood from the W. height. There are remains from the Geometric period to the Hellenistic, when this was a Ptolemaic naval station, while lower down was a Byzantine town. In the cemetery N. of the site is a fine Hellenistic stone-built tomb.

From Vái a poor road leads S.W. to *Toploú* (see above).

The Zakro road leaves the sea and winds through defiles and hills, passing several villages.—67 m. (107 km.) *Áno Zákro* (Zakro **C**). A Late Minoan villa c. ¾ m. farther on, partially underlying the Zakro road itself, yielded a wine press in 1965 and a pithos inscribed in Linear A (now in Herakleion). The road (dirt and very dusty in 1976, then rock) is being widened and realined and may be finished in 1977; it continues through bare schist foothills, passes the top of an impressive gorge, then winds steeply down to the sea.

72 m. *Káto Zákro*, a hamlet on a small bay, has a good shingle beach. Simple rooms are let at the café (Stelios Vassilakis). At the entrance to the hamlet (l.) is the **Palace of Zakro**. The site was partially investigated by D. G. Hogarth at the beginning of the century, and has been more thoroughly excavated by N. Platon since 1962. It consists of a terraced town with narrow streets, stepped and cobbled as at Gournia, and overlain by larger villas or palace dependencies, and below it a *Palace* of Late Minoan I period. This is often in part under water. It is similar in plan to the others, though smaller, and itself covers earlier remains (also probably Palatial). The palace seems to have suffered a sudden and terrible catastrophe which caused the buildings to collapse and burn. The inhabitants had had time to collect their most valuable portable belongings and escape, but though there was rebuilding in the town area, the palace was left largely undisturbed. It was neither restored nor looted (placed possibly under a 'tabu'?) and yielded to the excavators an almost full range of antiquities. Dr Platon links the destruction (not entirely plausibly) with the explosion of the island of Thera.

We enter by the remains of a Minoan road (Pl. 1) which came up from the harbour to the main entrance at the N.E. corner. To the left amid remains of the Old Palace excavation has revealed a bronze foundry. Thence it is easiest to start from the *Central Court*, c. 33 yds by 13, which was surrounded by façades in ashlar masonry (pseudo-isodomic) with timber beams. The squared blocks came from a quarry at Pelekita, c. 3 m. to the N. The WEST WING provided the cult centre, the walls being

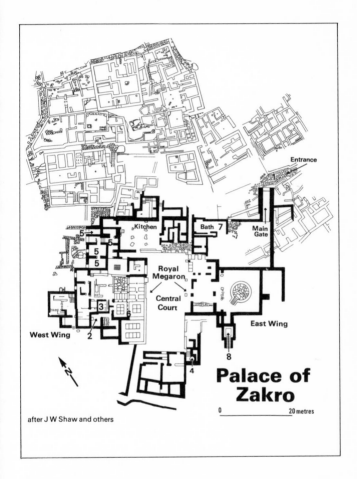

Palace of Zakro

Entrance

Kitchen   Bath 7   Main Gate

Royal Megaron

Central Court

East Wing

West Wing

5 5 5 3 2 6 4 8

N

0 _____ 20 metres

after J W Shaw and others

inscribed with double-axes. Here six ingots of bronze from Cyprus and three elephant tusks from Syria had fallen from the upper floor. Next to the small *Central Shrine* is a *Lustral Basin* (Pl. 3). The *Treasury* (Pl. 2) of the shrine yielded a remarkable collection of vessels in porphyry, alabaster, and basalt, now displayed in Herakleion (Arch. Mus. Gallery VIII). The *Archive Room* contained record tablets on shelves; most had been crushed but thirteen in Linear A were recovered. The *Magazines* (Pl. 5) should be noted. To the S. lies the so-called Hall of Ceremonies (Pl. 6) lit by a colonnaded light-well, and connecting with a *Banquet Hall* which was decorated with a frieze of painted stucco and yielded many drinking vessels.

The EAST WING, damaged by farming and by flooding and not completely uncovered, contained the private apartments, equipped with a bathroom (Pl. 7). A unique feature is the circular *Cistern* in a large hall served by a spring. The *Well of the Fountain* (Pl. 8), in an open court behind formed the main water supply of the palace, and there is another well (Pl. 4) farther W.

In the gorge of Zakro behind the Palace are caves with Early Minoan burials.

10   SITEIA TO IERAPETRA

ROAD, 40 m (64 km.), asphalt; a pleasant scenic alternative to the N. coast road.

The road (signposted Lithines) runs S. overlooking an open valley. A little out of Siteia, at a spot called *Manares*, is the first of a series of country villas of Late Minoan I date (1550–1450 B.C.) excavated by N. Platon. Note the staircase of two flights, the magazines, and, to the E. of the villa, a raised bank or dike, perhaps to protect the building from floods.—2½ m. *Piskokéfalo*. Here there has been excavated a Minoan sanctuary which contained many clay figurines, animal and human.

We may turn left at Piskokefalo for *Zoú* (2½ m.) where there is another large Minoan villa. It lies a little outside the village, to the S. By turning right in Piskokefalo we reach the village of *Akhládhia* (3¾ m.) where, at *Platyskinos*, stands a completely preserved Late Minoan III tholos tomb. About half an hour's walk N.E. of the village, at *Riza*, are two more Late Minoan I villas.

The main road continues through (6¼ m.) *Maronía*, rising gradually with wide views to the left. From an E.M. cave near here came a beautifully carved green stone pyxis with spirals (Her. Mus. case 7).—At (7½ m.) *Epáno Episkopi* we may diverge left to *Praisós* (3 m.). Ancient **Praisos,** capital of the Eteocretans (perhaps the descendants of the Minoan population) lies N. of the village, spread over three acropolis hills and the area between them. The remains, excavated by the British School at Athens at the beginning of this century, date from Late Minoan III to Hellenistic times and include tholos tombs of L.M. III and Geometric date to the S. of the acropolis, and rock-cut houses with a fine large Hellenistic one on the main, easternmost acropolis. The city was destroyed by Hierapytna in 155 B.C. (Strabo, X, 479, 12). Finds from the site include a fine L.M. III larnax, Archaic terracottas, small bronze models of armour and inscriptions in the Eteocretan language (6C–3C B.C.) in the Greek script but an unknown tongue, perhaps descended from Minoan Linear A (comp. B.S.A. 1901–02). A poor road rejoins the main road at Sikéa.

The main road rises gradually amid rolling country to the island's watershed between *Sikéa* and *Pappayiannádhes*, then descends through (15 m.) *Lithínai*. There are long straight stretches of new road in the Andromilos valley. As we round the last bend to the coast, range upon range of the Siteia Mountains extend to the W. rising to the heights of Thriptis. The road is rough for a mile of two through (21¼ m.) *Makriyialós*, but tavernas are springing up along the beach. We keep at low level near the coast. The sun is reflected by a myriad sheets of plastic used in the forcing of tomatoes. Occupation is agricultural and the hamlets small.—40 m. **Ierápetra**, see Rte 8.

II. KHANIA AND WESTERN CRETE

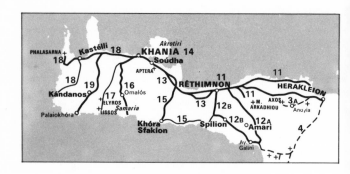

11   HERAKLEION TO RETHYMNO

A   By the New Road

The NEW HIGHWAY (48¾ m.) is now complete for 52 out of the 78 km. (no petrol stations). It may be joined S.W. of Herakleion and runs near the coast, affording an easy and scenic journey (followed by a few express buses), for much of the way along a deserted shore with intermittent access to the beach.

The road runs W. through (5 m.) *Linoperamata* (Akti Zeus, Apollonia Beach, both **A**) with oil storage tanks and cement works. By the Pandanassa Bridge is an Orthodox seminary and near the Palaiókastro Bridge remains of a medieval fort stand to seaward of Rogdiá. At 15 m. a road descends (r.; 1¾ m.) to the isolated Capsis Beach Hotel (**A**) on a headland of Ayia Pelayia. The road passes to seaward of Fódhele (see below) through which there is a link with the old road, and, at 21¼ m., there is another link through *Síses*. *Balion*, farther on, is a developing bathing place, named from the Bali café. We cross an approach road from Pérama (see below) just inland of *Pánormos* (Lavrys **B**), where, a little to the N.W., are the remains of an early Christian aisled basilica (5C) with an atrium, at the N. end of which is a baptistery. The church was perhaps the seat of the bishopric of Eleutherna at this period.—Just before (38½ m.) the *Yeropotamos Bridge* the White Mountains come into view. New hotels are being built near the point (at 42½ m.) where the unfinished highway provisionally rejoins the old road (comp. below).

B   By the Old Road

ROAD, 49 m. (79 km.), asphalt; buses frequently. The old road, slow and hilly, runs some way from the sea; this is described in greater detail since for those using public transport it alone gives access to most of the diversions.

The road quits Herakleion by the Pantokrator Gate. At 2 m. diverge left the road for Phaistos and the Mesara (Rte 4) and the access road to the new highway (see above). Just beyond *Gázi* we cross the new highway and leave (r.) a turning for *Rogdhiá* and *Ayia Pelayía* (anc. *Kytaion*), where new excavations have revealed Hellenistic, Archaic, and Late Minoan III buildings. Fódhele (see below) may be reached by branching left soon after Rogdhiá.—At 6¾ m. (11 km.) we leave the road to Tylissos and Anóyia (Rte 3B) on our left. The road now climbs high round the conical Mt Stromboli on the left amid boulder-strewn maquis. Just before the 15th km. post, a gap in the hills briefly affords a dramatic retrospective *View of the Bay of Herakleion.

The landscape becomes bare and craggy. A little way beyond (13 m.) *Marathós* a road descends right for *Fódhele* (4½ m.), the village where El Greco (Domenikos Theotokopoulos; c. 1541–1614) is thought on scanty evidence to have been born. The tradition was crystallized in 1934 when the University of Valladolid erected in his honour a bilingual inscription carved on slate from Toledo. The village lies amid orange groves and the church has two books with copies of his works.—We enter the nome of Rethymnon and descend gradually amid vineyards. *Drosiá* is a pleasant shady village, one of many along the twisting road. At 26 m. we join the road (l.) from Anóyia (see p. 64) viâ Garázon. We follow the Milopotamos valley.

34¼ m. *Pérama*. In the large village (955 inhab.) is the turning for Pánormos (4¼ m.; see above), off which, just out of Perama, is a turning for *Melidhóni*, beyond which is the celebrated stalactite cave where 370 Christians were smoked to death by the Turks in 1824.

35½ m. Turning (l.) for *Margarítes* (3 m.), a delightful potting village where all stages of the manufacture of clay vessels can be studied, and *Prinés* (4½ m.). After Margarites the road is unpaved and rough.

From Prinés ancient **Eleutherna** can be reached in ten minutes' walk by a path from the centre of the village. The acropolis stands at the end of a sharp, precipitous ridge, and is reached by a narrow rock causeway, guarded by a Byzantine tower. The acropolis fell to the Roman conqueror, Metellus Creticus (67 B.C.), only after a strong tower had been drenched with vinegar (Dio Cassius, XXXVI, 18, 2). Around the sides of the ridge are remains of the classical walls. In the W. side are vast Roman cisterns, while on the E. side a connecting conduit can be explored (torch advised). The cistern and conduit are not easy to find, and it is worth arranging for a guide in the village. From the site came an important Archaic statue (Herakleion Museum). Below the Acropolis to the N.W. (c. 15 min. walk) in the stream valley a remarkably fine and possibly Classical bridge can be seen, still in use. The road, still poor, continues through modern Eleutherna to join the main coastal road at Viran Episkopi (9½ m. from Prinés).

40½ m. *Virán Episkopí*. Here are a 16C Latin church and a 10C or early 11C Byzantine basilica, partly covered by a modern church, which also overlies the remains of a Hellenistic sanctuary (perhaps that of Artemis Diktynna). The basilica may have succeeded Sybrita as the seat of the medieval bishopric of Agrion after Sybrita was destroyed by the Saracens.

We soon reach the coast at Stavroménos and keep just inland of the new highway until it joins in from the right. Beyond the turn for Moni Arseniou (l.) is the El Greco Bungalow Hotel (**A**).—45½ m. *Plataniés* (Rithymna **A**). Here a road goes left through great groves of ancient

olives for *Amnátos* and up a rocky gorge to the monastery of **Arkádhi**
(9½ m.; *Arcadi,* 3R, **B**). Traditionally founded in the 11C, the
Monastery today (mainly late 17C) has as its chief architectural interest
the W. front of the Church (1587) in which elements of Classical,
Corinthian, and Baroque are extraordinarily well combined. The fame
of the place dates from November 1866 when it housed the powder
magazine of the insurgent Gen. Panos Koroneos. It was attacked by
Mustafa Kyrtli Pasha, the Turkish commissioner. After two days' siege,
the Abbot Gabriel blew up part of the building rather than surrender, so
that defendants and assailants alike perished (829 in all). In three of the
rooms in the gallery the relics of this event, including the Abbot's
vestments, are preserved. Today there are only 9 monks. The old
refectory is a melancholy place.—46¾ m. Road (signposted for Prassies)
for the Amari valley (see Rte 12). Several camping sites lie to seaward of
the main road.

49 m. **RETHYMNO** (ΡΕΘΥΜΝΟ; *Idaion, Xenia,* DPO, **B**; *Valari,
Park,* both without restaurant, **C**), or **Réthimnon,** a pleasant town
(15,000 inhab.), the capital of its nome as it was formerly of a Venetian
province, is considered by its inhabitants as the intellectual capital of the
island. It is built round a splendid sandy beach, dominated by the
eccentric lighthouse that guards the old Harbour. The relics of its
medieval past are being restored and a new harbour is under
construction. As an important market centre it is connected by bus with
the villages in the nome.

Minoan occupation is attested by Late Minoan III tombs at **Mastaba**, S.E. of
the main square. The Classical city was called *Rithymna.* The town flourished in
the Venetian period but was pillaged and burnt by Uluc-Ali Pasha's Turkish
corsairs in 1571. The Venetians then built the surrounding walls and fortress
(overlooking the sea on the N.W. of the town) but the Turks took it in 1645. The
town may have some faculties of the proposed university of Crete.

Just off the large main square is the *Public Garden,* formerly a
Turkish cemetery, where the varieties of trees and shrubs are labelled.
Each year in the last week of July the Cretan Wine Festival is held here.
At the rear of the garden animals are kept for display, confined in small
and inadequate cages.

A walk through the streets will reveal many charming Venetian house
façades and doorways. The houses with wooden balconies supported by
angular stays date from Turkish times; there are also several minarets.
From the N.W. corner of the square we pass down the narrow main
street. The 'Odeion' or concert hall has a 17C portal in the style of Seb.
Serlio from its Venetian days as the church (Santa Maria) of a religious
house. At the foot of the main street to the left is the *Arimondi Fountain,*
to the right the *Loggia,* one of the best Venetian buildings in Crete. Once
the army club, it is now the **Museum** (adm. fee; closed Mon and at
midday). The contents, from sites all over the province of Rethymnon,
are arranged as nearly as possible chronologically clockwise. Notable in
the wall-cases (l.) are goddess idols (L.M. III) from Sakhtouria and
Pangalokhori, and archaic heads and figurines from Axos. The central
cases, between good clay larnakes with octopus decoration, display fine
jewellery from Axos; Minoan necklaces; bronze axes from Amari and a
huge mirror from the Cave of Ida. Within the central columns, between
cases of good Minoan pottery from Mastaba and provincial red-figure
from various sites, is a remarkable case of coins, Classical to very late

Imperial, from various mints, Cretan and mainland. Behind a column, unfinished statue, half-worked with chisel marks; on the wall opposite the door, tympanum of 1531 in a very debased style. On the right side of the room an unexpected case of Egyptian statues, cartouches, and scarabs (not found in Crete); also Roman bronze finds from the Ay. Galini shipwreck, and some crude medieval sculpture.

The **Frourion** (adm. 7–3, free), or *Fortetza*, reached by steps alongside the modern prison, is imposing both in size and for the extent of the remains within. In the lower ward (l.) a deep well is reached by a sloping subterranean passage. Notable within the main enceinte are a little church, the Mosque with a fine dome, a lone date palm, and the battlemented or loop-holed ramparts. Judicious excavation and renovation have uncovered much interesting detail in the Venetian governor's quarters.

The main road continues W. to *Khaniá*, see Rte 13.

12   RETHYMNO TO AYIA GALINI

Some of the least known country in Crete extends S. of Rethymno. Lying between the peaks of the White Mountains and Mt. Ida, the region, though lower, is more broken, with upland valleys between smaller mountains. The inland areas are reminiscent of Provence, but in many places the S. coast falls into the sea in abrupt cliffs and is difficult of access, a characteristic it shares with Malta. The few roads reach the S. coast at the two main coastal plains.

A   Viâ the Amari Valley

ROAD, 41¼ m. (66 km.), asphalt.

The road (signposted Prassies) leads S. just E. of Rethymno, climbing to (7½ m.) *Prassiés*. In the village a path leads W. towards *Khromonastéri;* off this path (l.) in ½ hr we may reach Ayios Eftychios, a cross-in-square church dated by some authorities to the 12–13C, but quite possibly of the 11C. It has remains of frescoes in a flat linear style.—10 m. Road (r.) for Mírthios and *Gouledhianá* (3 m.) to the S. of which, at *Onithé* (possibly ancient *Phalanna*) N. Platon has excavated two Archaic houses (7–6C B.C.) and beyond which, at *Karé*, there is an early Christian basilica with mosaic pavements in the narthex. The apse of the nave has been restored.

We cross a bridge over a tributary of the Sfakoriako and enter the main valley. The main road climbs by continuous turns up the narrowing valley while oak and plane become more numerous. The valley becomes a mere gorge before the road reaches its summit.— 19½ m. *Apóstoloi*, with its 14–15C church stands at the head of the beautiful Amari Valley, lying between the Ida massif on the E. and Mt Kédros on the W. Here we may turn left to reach *Thrónos* with its frescoed church of the Dormition of the Virgin, overlying a basilica with mosaics; close by is the hill of ancient *Sybrita*, with fine walling and a gateway on the Thronos side.

An alternative road via Yerakári mav be taken round the W. side of the valley.

Returning to the valley road, we pass between *Yénna* (r.), where the church of Ay. Onouphrios has a frescoed Crucifixion of 1330, and *Kalóyeros* (l.), where two churches have 14C frescoes. There are others at (26 m.) the *Moni Asomáton* just off the road (r.) leading to Amari (3 m.). Part of this monastery has housed an Agricultural School since 1931. At *Amári*, the little 'capital' (166 inhab.) of an eparchy, the Asomatos has the earliest dated frescoes in Crete (1225). On the way, at Kharakas near Monastiraki, is a Minoan settlement with a Palatial-type building.

25½ m. *Vizári*. Among the olives 15 min. W. of the village are the remains of a large Roman town where there is a mosaic floor (A.D. 250–300) and an early Christian basilica with the foundations well preserved. Two Arab (Saracen) coins were found in its destruction debris.—27 m. *Fourfourás* tumbles down the hill on the left. At (31½ m.) *Níthavris*, which looks W. towards Mt Kedros, we meet the road from the W. side of the valley.

This road, the right branch at Apóstoloi (see above), passes *Méronas, Vríses* (just W. of the 13C church of *Smilés*), and *Áno Méros*.

We may continue S. to join the road between Timbáki and Ayia Galini, described in Rte 5.—41¼ m. *Ayía Galíni*, and the alternative return road viâ Spili, see Rte 12B.

B   Viâ Spíli

ROAD, 38 m. (asphalt). Bus 2 or 3 times daily.

We leave Rethymno by the park; the road (unsignposted in 1979) climbs by turns to a better width, then runs S.—About a mile before (7 m.) *Arménoi*, an LM III cemetery (signposted; 100 yds up a new road, r., and amid oak trees, l.) yielded numerous larnakes with bull motifs in 1970, now in Khania Museum. The road rises gently in attractive country. At 13 m. the way divides.

The right branch runs W. amid a pastoral landscape with barley fields and flowers to (18 m.) *Ayios Ioánnis*. Here it again turns S. through the narrow ravine of the Kótsifas to (22 m.) *Sellía*, a compact village commanding an attractive coastal plain. A little before the village a new road diverges (l.), crosses the ravine, and descends viâ Mírthios to *Plakiás* (6 m.; Alianthos C, and others). The last half-mile is rough, but there is a magnificent beach.—From Sellia W. to Frangokastello and *Khora Sfakion*, see p. 111.

The main road continues left. About 1 m. farther on a road branches right through *Koxaré* (½ m.) and the magnificent Kourtaliotiko gorge of the Megapotamos to *Préveli* monastery (8 m.), finely situated on the sea. Its aid to allied soldiers in 1941 is commemorated by a gift of silver candlesticks from Britain.—From (15½ m.) *Mixórrouma* there is a minor road to *Labiní* (l.; 1 m.), with its interesting frescoed church of the Panayia (14C and later).—18¾ m. *Spíli* is a lovely village. The road runs in the long valley between Mt Kédros (5829 ft) on the N. and Sidérotas (3726 ft) on the S. through Akoúmia.—Beyond (31 m.) *Mélambes* (1010 inhab.) we round the E. end of Vouthála and descend to the sea.—38 m. *Ayía Galíni* (Astoria, Acropolis C, and many smaller; tavernas; rooms), anciently *Soulia*, is a village (500 inhab.) with a tiny harbour. In summer its charms attract greater numbers than it can comfortably absorb. The rocky beach at the mouth of the Platys (c. 1 m. E.) has a camping-site.

There is a 7 a.m. ferry-boat (Mon, Wed, Fri westward; Tues, Thurs, Sat eastward) between Ayia Galini and Ayia Roumeli, making calls at Plakias, Frangokastello, Khora Sfakion, and Loutro. On Sun the journey is made both ways but without intermediate calls.

13   RETHYMNO TO KHANIA

ROAD, 36 m. (58 km.), part of the N. coast highway. Buses frequently all day. The old road, narrow and winding and now superseded for all but local traffic, made two wide loops in hilly terrain to the S., adding c. 10 m. to the distance. The E. loop serves Atsipópoulo, a picturesque village, and Episkopi; the second, beyond Vrises, passes through Néo Khorió.

The new road at first follows the coast. We cross the Yerani bridge, beneath which is a cave, and round a bend to see the White Mountains ahead. There are frequent lay-bys for the (deserted) beaches. Beyond the nome boundary the old and new roads coincide for some miles. Off to the left (c. 3 m.) is *Lake Kournás*, the only lake in Crete, set at the foot of Mt Trypali.—12¾ m. *Yeoryioúpolis* (on the old road; r.) occupies the site of ancient *Amphimalla*, a port of Lappa, the powerful city in the hills to the S.W.—We follow an inland valley dotted with villages and cypress clumps, through which runs the Tris Almiri river.—18 m. *Vríses* (ΒΡΥΣΕΣ; l.; junction with the old road), a delightful stopping-place beneath tall plane trees, has a memorial of the 1898 rising. Here diverges the road to Khóra Sfakíon (Rte 15).

The bare cuttings of the new highway resemble pale chocolate layer cake, argillaceous bands alternating with rock. We leave the peninsula of Vamos on our right, running between the White Mountains and the sea, which we approach near (25 m.) *Kalíves*. The road passes between two large Turkish fortresses (see below). At 29½ m. the approach road to Aptera (l.) climbs and after 1¼ m. divides: left for the deserted Turkish fort (*View) and right for the abandoned monastery that marks the ancient city. **Aptera**, one of the largest ancient cities of Crete, is said to take its name (Wingless Ones) from the Sirens who were defeated in a musical contest by the Muses, plucked off their wings and, drowning in the bay below, formed the little islets visible there. The city flourished in Classical and Roman times (its coins are common) and was the seat of a bishopric in the early Christian period. Remains of monuments to be seen include a small Doric *Temple of Apollo* near the Roman *Theatre*, a Hellenistic *Temple of Demeter*, a double temple or *Treasury*, and fine Classical defence *Walls* in the valley on the N.E. of the site. The vast underground Roman cisterns, having three great vaulted arcades of five bays, are comparable with those at Pleuron in N.W. Greece.

On the promontory of *Kalámi*, below the fortress of Aptera, is a Venetian fortress, taken by the Turks in 1715 and used, together with another fort on the islet opposite, to guard the entrance to Soudha Bay. Still called *Itzedin*, it is now a prison. The main road continues along the S. shore of Soudha Bay, passing the attractive modern Naval Hospital.—32 m. **Soúdha** (*Parthenon, Knossos*, both **D**), a major Greek naval base and a NATO harbour, is also the port for Khania. The great *Bay* will take the largest ships and is well protected. Just off the main road (r.) is the large main square with many cafés, and beyond, a spacious waterfront. Near the head of the bays is a *British Military Cemetery* containing graves (mostly Commonwealth) of 1497 men who fell in May 1941 during the Battle of Crete. Among them is that of John Pendlebury, the English archaeologist, shot by the Germans as a member of British Intelligence. Hither in 1963 were transferred from the Consular cemetery 19 graves from the First World War and 51 other graves dating back to 1897.—36 m. (58 km.) **Kkaniá**, see Rte 14.

14 KHANIÁ

KHANIA (XANIA), officially *Ta Khania,* the capital of Crete, with 40,600 inhab., is a pleasant town, well provided with squares and gardens, and preserving many features of its Venetian and Turkish past. It has a museum with finds from various parts of Western Crete and is a good centre for excursions to the sites from which they came.

Airport at Akrotiri (*Sternes*), 10 m. E.; services to Athens twice daily.
Car Ferry services from *Soudha*, 4 m. E., to Piraeus; other steamers to Rethymno and Herakleion; to Kythera and Gytheion. Shipping Offices in Khatsimikhaili Yiannari and Khalidhon.

Hotels. Kidon (Pl. a), Plat. El. Venizelou, 110 R.; **Xenia** (Pl. b), by the sea, with swimming pool, both DPO, **A. Doma** (Pl. i), small, in a restored historic mansion, 124 El. Venizelou; **Porto Veneziano** (Pl. j), on the old harbour; **Samaria** (Pl. m), Khidonias; **Lissos** (Pl. e), 68 Dhimokratias, without rest., **B. Lucia** (Pl. k), Akti Koundourioti; **Kriti** (Pl f), Foka/Kiprou; **Diktynna** (Pl. g); **Khania** (Pl. h). 18 Plat. 1866; **Cyprus** (Pl. d), 17 Tzanakaki, **Hellenis** (Pl. n), 68 Tzanakaki, these **C**.
Restaurants. *Faros, Delfini, Kavouria* on the harbour; and in Plateia 1866 and 1897; also in Khalépa near the shore.
Post Office, Stratigou Tsanakaki.—O.T.E. CENTRE, adjacent.
Buses from Bus Station to *Rethymno* and *Herakleion*; from Plateia 1866 to local villages.
Commemoration of Battle of Crete (Festival of Dancing), 27-29 May.

History. This was the site of ancient *Kydonia*, a place-name found in the Linear B tablets of Knossos. Minoan occupation is attested by the settlement discovered on the Kastelli, dating right through from Neolithic times to Classical, with the L.M. IIIb period representing the zenith. Late Minoan III tombs have been found in the area of the Law Courts. Kydonia in post-Minoan times was one of the three leading cities of Crete (with Knossos and Gortyn). The Venetians occupied it in 1252 (calling it La Canea) and, apart from a short period when it fell to the Genoese (1267–90), held it until 1645. Under them a notable building programe was executed, at first on the Kastelli with a Cathedral and the Palace of the Rector, which area was walled around between 1320 and 1366. The raids of Barbarossa, the corsair Turk, in 1537, compelled Venice to fortify the whole town. The walls and bastions were fronted by a great moat up to 50 yds wide. On its S. side this moat ran approximately along the line of Skalidhi and Hatzimikhali Giannari Streets. After a siege the city fell to the Turks in 1645. It became the seat of the Pashalik and in the 19C the old Kastelli was the capital of the island. There were several Cretan insurrections in this period but it was not until 1898 that Turkish rule was ended.

Prince George of Crete entered the city and governed the island as High
Commisioner under the Allied Powers (Britain, France, and Russia). During this
period of Crete's independence (until 1913) and since, Khaniá has remained the
island's capital. It was captured by the Germans after the Battle of Crete in May
1941 and liberated in 1945.

The focal point of the town is the large open space in front of the
cruciform covered *Market* together with the *Plateia 1897* to the W.
whence Odhos Khatsimikhaili Yiannari (with a fine minaret) leads W. to
the other important square, *Plateia 1866* (good view of the White
Mountains). To the N. lies the Venetian walled town with its dilapidated
streets. Odhos Khalidhon leads N. towards the harbour. On the left is
the Venetian church of *San Francesco*, crudely constructed with a
vaulted nave and narrow aisles, and having side chapels on the
ecclesiastical S. (The church in fact has a reverse orientation). A Turkish
fountain in the adjoining garden survives from its days as the Mosque of
Yusuf Pasha. Since 1962 the church has housed the **Archaeological
Museum** (temp. closed in 1979). We enter by the W. door. The
progression is roughly chronological from W. to E., though some
movement of exhibits is to be expected.

To the left of the door, Cases 1-3 display fine Early Minoan pottery
from the Platyvola cave, excavated since 1966. Note the inscription of
1617 above Case 2. The next group (Cases 4-7 & 9) continues the ceramic
ware from Platyvola, from Perivolia, and from the Kastelli excavations
in Khania. Case 8 contains Neolithic pottery from the Kumarospilio, a
cave on Akrotiri, also Cycladic vases from the Tsivourakis collection.
Farther on, in the left aisle, Cases 10, 11 & 13 contain Minoan vases and
imported Cypriot ware from Kastelli Khania, while Case 14 (in front)
holds necklaces from various sites.

In the centre the clay *Larnakes include magnificent polychrome
examples from the cemetery near Armenoi, S. of Rethymno. One with
double axes has bulls of cartoon aspect. In the S.W. corner are further
cases of fine Minoan ware: Case 15 includes a large painted krater from
Soudha; Case 16, mirrors, swords, and axes from tombs in the town and
from near-by Samona. In Cases 17-21 recent pottery finds include very
fine L.M. III vases from a tomb at Kalami, particularly a pyxis with a
man playing a lyre to birds. An unnumbered case by the S.W. door
contains the Linear A tablets found in Kastelli.

Returning to the N. aisle: Cases 22-23, Protogeometric pottery from
tombs at Nokhia (Modi), and (24) from Kavoussi. The Sanctuary
contains 'the Philosopher of Elyros', a heroic Roman copy of a Greek
orator, and a vigorous Roman mosaic portraying Neptune and Amy-
mone. On the S. side, Colossal head of Hadrian from the Diktynnaion.
Returning along the S. side: Cases 26-27. Archaic figurines from Axos.
Case 31, Black-figure vases from Phalasarna. On a pillar: plaque,
Nymph and Satyr, with Erotes, from Polyrrhenia. Case 32, Bronze
mirrors. Beyond the Renaissance S. portal, Case 37 contains good
Roman glass from Kissamos and from various tombs.

In the body of the Nave, Sculpture, mainly Classical: *Youth with
delicate features from the Asklepieion at Lissos; opposite, Pan from
Hyrtakina; well-preserved obese figure of Herakles from Hydramias;
Artemis from the Diktynnaion; Asklepios; Hygieia from Aptera;
Aphrodite from Kydonia, several charming marble statues of children
and a table from Lissos.

We reach the peaceful OUTER HARBOUR, protected by a long Venetian mole with a Turkish lighthouse, but now largely deserted for Soudha.

On the quay to the right are the Plaza hotel, the external staircase of which incorporates a Venetian/Turkish fountain, and the *Mosque of the Janissaries*, built in 1645, now restored as a tourist pavilion (information bureau and restaurant). Continuing round the foot of Kastelli hill (comp. below) we come to the INNER HARBOUR, fronting which is the vaulted *Arsenal*, constructed towards 1600. A Yacht Marina is under construction. Part of the *Sabbionara Bastion*, to the N.E., and the *East Wall* are preserved. In the quarter behind stands AYIOS NIKOLAOS, a Dominican church of the Venetians, transformed by the Turks into the Imperial Mosque of Sultan Ibrahim when its tower became a minaret; the Orthodox church claimed it in 1918. The galleried nave has a coffered ceiling. The great plane-tree in the square is a Turkish survival as the inevitable plaque recording 1821 recalls. The maze of tiny streets to the E. forms the most picturesque corner of the town. *Ayioi Anargyroi* (16C) contrived to remain an Orthodox church under both Venetians and Turks. The little church of *San Rocco*, farther W., bears a Latin inscription of 1630.

Stretches of the *Inner Wall*, the original 14C rampart, may be seen between Sfaka and Kanevaro streets. The Castello itself (or Kastelli) has suffered from bombing and military occupation and little remains on the hill; at 37 Lithinoi the doorway of the Venetian *Archives* survives, with an inscription of 1623. Greco-Swedish excavations since 1966 on the hill in and around Plat. Ay. Aikaterini brought to light buildings that had suffered destruction by fire in LM I as well as houses dated to Late Minoan IIIB; a scarab of Thothmes III was found out of stratigraphical context, and there were pieces of pottery imported from Cyprus. Clay tablets bearing Linear A inscriptions were found in 1972–73. Off Zampeliou is a *Gate* bearing the arms of the Venieri family, dated 1608.

Akti Koundouriotis, lined with tavernas and the venue of the vòlta, leads to the left round the Outer Harbour to the *Naval Museum of Crete* (daily 10–12 & 5-8; fee), in which episodes of Greek naval history are illustrated by ship models and photographs; there are few genuine relics. To the N.W., on and behind the waterfront, picturesque Venetian houses extend to the Bastion of *San Salvatore*. The church of the same name lies behind. From the Xenia Hotel we may follow the *Western Wall* to the *Bastion of San Demetrio*, backed by the great circular mound of the *Lando• Bastion*. These were all constructed by 1549.

From the centre Odhos Stratigou Tsanakaki leads S.E. past the Post Office and the *Public Gardens* to the interesting **Historical Museum and Archives** in a quarter of 19C villas and fasionable apartments. Hence we may reach the former *Palace of the Governor* and the *House of Eleutherios Venizelos* in the plesant KHALÉPA quarter on the E. edge of the town. This ends, beyond the Doma hotel (in 1912 the British Embassy to independent Crete and in 1942 the German Commandant's house) and a taverna, in a quaint waterside village with tanneries, a cottage industry producing sheep and goat skins and chamois-leather.

Behind Khalépa runs the road to the **Akrotiri**, the limestone peninsula on the N.E. of Khaniá that protects Soudha Bay.—3 m. Road (l.) for *Profitis Ilias*, the hill where the Greek standard was raised by insurgents in 1897 in the teeth of an international naval bombardment. A statue of Eleutheria (Liberty) commemorating the event has been destroyed by lightning, but the tomb of Eleutherios Venizelos (1864–1936) is impressive in its simplicity. Three popular

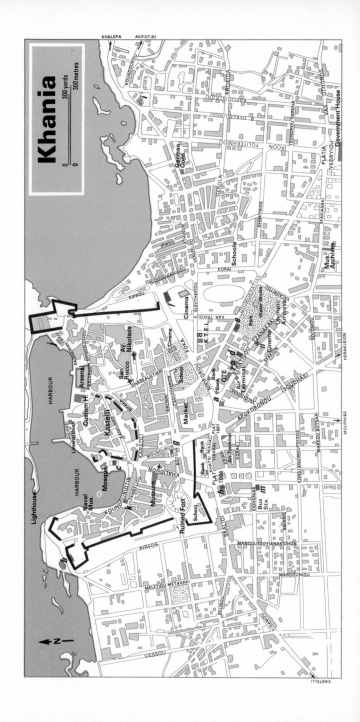

restaurants command a fine view over the Bay.—A little beyond this fork is another where we keep left, leaving the Stérnes (airport) road. At (5 m.) *Kounoupidhianá* we keep right for *Kabáni* and (10¼ m.) the monastery of *Ayia Triádha*. Erected in the early 17C and sometimes called after its Venetian founder Tzangarol, it has a fine gateway (1632) and a church built in Renaissance style (1632), the campanile being a little later. A walk of c. 1 hr to the N. will bring us to the Monastery of *St John of Gouverneto*, whose cave is near by (festival on 7 Oct).

15 KHANIA (OR RETHYMNO) TO KHORA SFAKION

ROAD, 43 m (67 km.), asphalt. *Vríses*, the point of divergence, is almost equidistant (18 m.) between Khaniá and Rethymno; thence it is a further 25 m. to *Khóra Sfakíon*. Buses infrequently from Khania, daily from Rethymno.

From Khaniá (or Rethymno) to *Vríses*, see Rte 12. The narrow road winds S. and, beyond (22 m.) *Alíkambos*, climbs through rough unattractive country. Serpentine but rarely steep, it runs deeper into the E. ranges of the White Mts without habitation through shaly defiles. At the top of a zigzag climb we see below the PLAIN OF ASKYPHOU (2395 ft), where the tiny square fields interspersing the villages are dominated by a ruined Turkish castle on an isolated hill. The Sfakiots were notorious for their local vendettas and the villages and even neighbouring houses occupy fortified mounds.

The road goes round the W. side of the plain, then climbs by a ladder of zigzags to (30½ m.). **Pétres**. At (32 m.) the top of the pass a rough narrow road diverges left to Asféndou (3¾). Our road runs fairly level through *Nímbros* above a natural cleft in the mountain range. We emerge high above the Libyan Sea with superb *Views of the coast to the E. as a series of vertiginous turns takes the road down nearly 2500 in a few miles. At the foot the road divides. The right branch leads down into (43 m.) **Khóra Sfakion** (ΧΩΡΑ ΣΦΑΚΙΩΝ; *Xenia* C), the tiny capital of the Sfakiots, famed for their independence through all periods of Cretan history. Through its narrow mountain approaches during the four nights 28-31 May 1941 more than 10,000 troops were withdrawn to be embarked by the Royal Navy for Egypt. The place is frequented for bathing, mainly by Greeks.

A desperate rough zigzag can be seen rising to *Anópolis* (7½ m.). Excursions can be made by boat E. to Ay. Galini (Rte 12) or W. to Loutro and Ay. Roúmeli for the Gorge of Samaria (Rte 16).

To FRANGOKÁSTELLO AND SELLÍA (RETHYMNO). We return to the road junction (comp. above) and continue E. The road was well engineered in the early 70s but unfinished and already deteriorating in 1979. We soon come to *Komitádhes* (½ m.), where the church of Ay. Yeoryios has fine frescoes, painted by Ioannes Pagomenos (1313; this is the earliest of seven churches known to have been painted by him). The road runs along a coastal slope below the mountains and is very rough, but villages every mile or two have cafés.—At (5 m.) *Kapsodhásos* we turn right (poor track) for **Frangokástello** (1¼ m.), which has been visible on the shore for some time. There is a fine beach and three tavernas with rooms. The great fortress, built by the Venetians in 1371, is square in plan with square towers at the corners. Though imposing with its battlements it is a mere shell. It is claimed that at dawn on or near 17-18 May each year phantoms dance round the fort representing the army of Khatzimikhailis which was overwhelmed here by the Turks in 1828. The phenomenon is so well attested over a long period that sceptics have been moved to suggest a mirage effect reflected from Libya.

To make the round trip to Rethymno we continue E. The dirt road serving Frangokástello loops back to the 'main' road which climbs. Between (8¼ m.) *Skalotí* and *Argoulés*, the next village, the road is new and broad, but (in 1979) unsurfaced, but it deteriorates as we enter the nome of Rethymno in rough terrain. The scenery improves as we climb above lovely sandy (but hardly accessible) beaches.—11¼ m. *Rodhákinon* has two parts on either side of a ravine. The road between is very rough. The coast becomes increasingly steep-to, with the road ever higher above the water. A vicious pass crosses a promontory of wild crags, then the landscape alters as we descend by gentler turns to an attractive coastal plain.—16¼ m. *Sellía*, and thence to Rethymno, see Rte 12b.

16   KHANIA TO OMALO AND THE GORGE OF SAMARIA

This excursion may be made by car, or by bus (twice daily), to the Tourist Pavilion on the Omaló Plain, whence the descent on foot through the Gorge to Ayia Roúmeli on the coast takes about 5-6 hrs. From Ayia Roúmeli, where the Kapheneion on the beach offers accommodation, three boats a day in summer ply E. tó Loutro and Khora Sfakion (whence there is a morning bus viâ Vryses to Khaniá, comp. Rte. 15) or W. to Palaiókhora (see p. 116). In summer the organized excursion takes 14 hrs. A coach leaves Khania c. 6 a.m. for Omalo and picks up in the evening from Khora Sfakion.

We leave Khaniá by the main Kastelli road to the W., and after 1 m. turn left (signposted Omalo) along an avenue of eucalyptus trees.—3 m. *Vamvakópoulo* has the appearance of a villa suburb. Groves of oranges surround the huge prison of '*Phylakes*' (r.). Along the road tall reeds alternate with Mediterranean pine and cypresses.—5 m. *Ayiá* has a 14C church with three naves. By the Alikianós turn (comp. Rte 17) is a memorial ossuary to partisans killed by the Germans.—At (9½ m.) *Fournés* the road forks. The right branch goes direct to Lákkoi (see below) or we may take the left fork to visit *Mesklá* (4 m. S. in the Keritis valley), where the Byzantine church of the Metamorphosis (Transfiguration) has frescoes of 1303, while mosaics from an ancient Temple of Venus underlie another church at the S. end of the village. Another fine church with Byzantine frescoes is that of Christ the Saviour. From the village there is a steep path (c. 1 hr) up to Lákkoi.

The direct road crosses the Keritis and quits the valley, climbing in great zigzags. Olives are cultivated in terraces as the view increases in grandeur.—15¼ m. *Lákkoi* tumbles down the mountainside in picturesque clusters of red-roofed houses with white walls. The climb continues across bleak stony uplands strewn with aromatic rock-plants. A succession of steep zigzags climbs the mountainside to a surprisingly level enclosed pass. A little farther on, at an altitude of 3250 ft, a plaque records the death on 28 Feb 1944 of the New Zealander, Dudley Perkins, and a Greek partisan companion. Perkins (better known as Kapitan Vassilios) had escaped from Crete in 1942 and returned from the Middle East an an agent. The road again climbs amid stunted fir trees to a summit (3935 ft), then makes a short steep descent in view of the

Volakias peaks to (24¼ m.) the *Omaló Plain*, where wheat and vegetables are grown in the spring and summer, though it is too high for the olive (3610 ft). Here the Cretan leaders met in Apr-May 1866 to petition the Sultan against new taxation. Their approaches to foreign consuls precipitated the Cretan revolt. We enter the plain from the E.; the top of the gorge is at the S. On the way we pass a rocky path (l.) leading to an Alpine Club hut for climbs in the White Mts. The *Xenia Tourist Pavilion* (Rfmts; 3 rooms) stands above the head of the gorge, now incorporated into a Regional Park, in which animals and plants alike are strictly protected.

The ****Gorge of Samaria** (Τὸ Φαράγγι τῆς Σαμαριᾶς) is said to be the longest true gorge in Europe (c. 11 m.) and throughout is a region of outstanding beauty. The initial descent is by the *Xilóskalo* (Wooden Staircase). In parts the walls come very close together, rising sheer for nearly 1000 feet. The walk itself presents no problems, for there is water and a footpath all through and four guards patrol the gorge. This is the only region where the Cretan agrimi or wild goat is to be found in its natural habitat. About half-way through is *Samaria*; the village is now deserted though some houses still stand. Farther down are the 'Iron Gates', where the walls of the gorge are only a few yards wide.

We emerge at *Ayia Roúmeli*, the site of ancient *Tarrha*, which has produced fine Roman glass. The ancient temple on the site of the Church of the *Panayia*, was probably that of Artemis.

17   FROM KHANIA TO SOÚIA

ROAD, 43½ m. (70 km.), asphalt to beyond Prinés, poor beyond.

From Khaniá to Ayia, see Rte 16. Beyond Ayia, at 6¾ m. we turn right for (7½ m.) *Alikianoú*, crossing the Keritis, but before reaching the village turn off left up the river valley. The village church (Ay. Yeoryios) has frescoes of 1430 by Paul Probatus.—9¾ m. *Skinés* (Tavernas) is a pretty village with fine trees and citrus groves. At Khliaró the road begins to climb into the well-watered foothills of the White Mountains. The top of the first pass is reached before (16 m.) *Nea Roúmata*.— Beyond (19 m.) *Prassés* the road climbs again with wide views towards the top peaks of the White Mts. (l.) After a further summit it enters the enclosed valley of *Ayia Iríni*.—At (29 m.) *Epanokhori* comes the first sight of the Libyan Sea. A continuous long descent from *Prinés*, a little farther on, becomes slower beyond Kambanos where the surface starts to deteriorate. At a broad unsignposted T-junction the road divides (r. to Palaiokhora, see below). Hereabouts are the unexplored ruins of **Elyros**, the most important ancient city of S.W. Crete. It flourished under the Romans and Byzantines (when it was the seat of a bishop) but was destroyed in the 9C Saracen invasions. Traces of walls, a theatre, and an aqueduct may be seen.

The left turn brings an immediate steep and winding descent through Moní.—43 m. (70 km.) *Soúia,* where is ancient *Syia*, the port of Elyros; remains of an aqueduct and baths survive and in the village church there is a mosaic pavement of a 6C basilica with representations of deer, peacocks, and interwoven vines. An hour's walk W. of Soúia at *Ayios Kyrkos* is ancient **Lissos**, the port of Hyrtakina to the N.; a good deal of the *Asklepieion* is preserved, including mosaics inside the temple. The ancient water supply for the building passed under the floor to feed a fountain. On a terrace to the N.E. are remains of baths; other buildings, including perhaps a waiting place for the sick, lie to the N. In excavations in the temple, important finds were made, including statuettes of the 3C B.C. and, more recently, a Theatre has come to light.

To PALAIOKHÓRA, 15 m., poor but motorable road. From the T-junction (see above) the road enters *Rhodhováni*.—4 m. *Teménia* (Inn) stands at the junction of another poor road from Kandanos.—9 m. *Azoyires* is near the site of ancient HYRTAKINA, where walls survive and a Temple of Pan has been explored.—At 13 m. the main Palaiokhóra road (Rte 19) is reached.

18   FROM KHANIA TO KASTELLI AND THE W. COAST

ROAD (asphalt) to (26 m.) *Kastelli,* continuing to (31½ m.) *Platanos.* Motorable track to *Phalasarna.* The new highway, not yet completed, runs close and parallel most of the way to Kastelli.

The road runs W. along the coast over which the German airborne invasion of 1941 swept in from bases in Attica.—1¼ m. *Aptera Beach* (Bungalow Hotel **C**). To the left of the road the German monument to their 2nd Parachute Regiment takes the aggressive form of a diving eagle. The 'Golden Beaches' of the National Tourist Organisation (signposted EOT), with camping sites, are approached by broad by-roads. *Glaros Beach* and *Kalamáki Beach* are passed amid haphazard development along the sandy Khaniá Bay. The bathing is not always safe. The new Panorama Hotel is well sited above the road. The island of *Ayión Theodóron,* prominent off the coast, is one of several reserves for the Cretan wild goat.—6½ m. *Plataniás* (taverna) has spread from its flat-topped hill down to the shore. We cross the Kerítis amid groves of bamboo and wind through small orange groves, each protected by high bamboo windbreaks against the meltémi.—10 m. *Máleme* (Crete Chandris, 400 R., **A**) has a German military cemetery (l.) and, a little farther on, near the hotel, the military airport which was the focus of the Battle of Crete in May 1941.

A new bridge over another torrent has superseded two Bailey bridges (r.) that did service for thirty years. At (12 m.) *Tavronítis* (cafés), a centre of melon growing, a road branches left for Palaiokhóra (see p. 116). Beyond *Kamisianá* (tavernas) we cut across the base of the RHODOPOÚ PENINSULA, on which *Kolimvári,* the first village, with its monastery is prominent. The Moní Goniás, or Hodegetria, was founded in 1618, though the buildings date from 1662 and later. There are fine 17C icons, including one signed by the Cretan artist, Konstandinos Palaiokapas (1637).—14¾ m. The Rose Marie Hotel (**D**, small, Apr-Oct) stands at the turn.

At the N.E. corner of the peninsula is ancient *Diktynna,* reached by turning off right viā Kolimvári to *Afráta,* whence it is a walk of some hours. A better way of reaching it is to take a motor-boat from Kolimvári. There was a city here with a famous Sanctuary of Artemis Diktynna (a temple of the 2C A.D. built on the site of earlier Hellenisitc and Classical temples.).—At 15 m. on the Kastelli road a road branches off right for Koumouli and *Rhodhopoú* (3¾ m.) from which a track leads N. (2. hrs on foot) to Ayios Ioánnis, venue of a pilgrimage on 29 August.

The main road, here narrow and tortuous, threads a natural gap in the hills. Suddenly the Gulf of Kissamou, with the plain of Kastelli, bursts on the view (superb *Panorama in the evening). To the S., as we descend, craggy dolomitic mountains fill the sky, and ahead the long line of Gramvousa rears out of the sea. We pass the turning (r.) for *Nopígia* on the coast, near which was ancient *Mithymna*.—23 m. *Kaloudhianá*; by-road for Topolia, see below. The plain is densely planted with olives.

26 m. (42 km.) **Kastélli Kissámou** (*Kastell* C) lies to seaward of the road, a long straggle of buildings, set back from its fine sandy beach. Here was ancient *Kissamos*, the port of Polyrrhenia. Kastelli was a thriving Venetian town, fortified in the 16C. The *Museum*, not much more than an Apotheke, situated below the Post Office in the main square, contains local finds, notably a good grave relief and a marble satyr. Two small fishing harbours lie isolated to the W. of the town; one of these is being developed.

To POLYRRHENIA (bus twice daily). From the main road a wide triangle opens into Odhos Episkopou Anth. Leledake (signposted only to the Police Station) which, after an inconspicuous start, is asphalted for 3 m. and motorable through two hamlets to (4¼ m.) the foot of *Ano Palaiókastro*. Stepped, tortuous, and possibly ancient stone roads (best to right) lead in 15 min. through the village to the unexpected site of **Polyrrhenia**, a plateau on which stands a church. A clear Roman inscription is built low into the W. wall. Blocks and roof tiles lie around from the Temple, the fine lower courses of whose side wall still support the modern cemetery. In the extensive walling on the Acropolis above, Archaic and Classical masonry remains despite considerable Frankish or Turkish rebuilding. Polyrrhenian coins show the worship of several deities, including Diktynnaian Artemis.

FROM KASTELLI TO TOPÓLIA AND KOUNÉNI. We take the Khania road and, at (3 m.) *Kaloudhianá* (comp. above), turn inland up the valley to (8 m.) *Topólia*. Just over a mile S. of the picturesque village, a path leads up to the right in 5 min. to the *Cave of Ay. Sofia* (no difficulty of access). It has fine stalactites and was used in Neolithic, Early and Late Minoan, Classical, Hellenistic, and Roman times, and now has a small church within.—A dirt road continues through magnificent chestnut woods up the Giflos valley, leaving on the right a branch for Vlátos and on the left one to Strovlès, and comes to (15 m.) *Élos* (2625 ft). It now turns W. to (18 m.) *Kefáli*, where the two churches are frescoed (Sotiros, 1320; Athanasios, 1343). Here a turning runs S. in c. 1 m. to *Kounéni*, where the church of Ay. Yeoryios (a few minutes on foot above the village to the right of the road) has frescoes of 1284. When the ceiling fell in, the villages repaired it, jumbling the scenes, but good pieces survive. The original sketches in the apse form an interesting comparison with the frescoes themselves (contrast the narrow jaws with the fully painted heads). In the fields below the road, a few mins. S. of the village (path), the church of Mikhail Arkhangelos has early 14C frescoes, notably the Fall of Jericho and the Presentation in the Temple.

The adventurous may continue (6 or 7 m. farther) S.W. from Kouneni to reach the coast at the *Moni Khrysoskalítissa* (our Lady of the Golden Stair). Those without sin are reputed to be able to see which of the 90 steps is made of gold.

Beyond Kastelli the main road continues W. past a small cave church and after a while turns inland from the gulf, passing through the scattered contiguous villages of Ayios Yeóryios, Zerviá, and Kamártsos.—31½ m. *Plátanos*. Road works W. of the village in 1970 uncovered a chamber tomb containing Protogeometric pottery, the first time it had been found this far W.

At the end of the village a stone road is signposted for *Falásarna* (3 m.). The road soon comes in view of the sea, affording a lovely *Panorama with the magnificent W. side of Gramvousa to the N., a thick olive plain to the S., and a long sandy beach in between. The last km. of bad dirt road needs care. Ancient **Phalasarna** is marked, beyond a lone café, by a plaque, necessarily since there is little to see save a rock-cut throne, some walling, and overgrown beddings in the rock. The city was independent and had a temple to Diktynnaian Artemis. Its cemetery has started to yield black-figured pottery, some of Corinthian origin, of the 6C B.C. Here best of all in West Crete, the rising of the land since ancient times is demonstrated, the old sea line being up to 28ft higher than the present one. This tilting has brought the ancient harbour remains 150 yds inland and made them even less intelligible.

Beyond Platanos the rough unmade road climbs to a high col with superb views down to Phalasarna, then descends to (37 m.) *Sfinári*, an attractive village with a fine beach. The road is under construction to the Moni Khrysoskalitissa (see p. 115).

19   KHANIA TO PALAIOKHORA

ROAD, 48 m. (77 km.), asphalt. Bus once or twice daily.

To (12½ m.) *Tavronítis*, on the Kastelli road, see Rte 18. The Kándanos road goes left in the village and follows the W. bank of a broad torrent in a lush valley.—16 m. *Voukoliés* is a large centre with a plateia shaded by plane-trees. The road crosses a col into a parallel valley to the W., for a while running along a ridge with views on either side and back to the sea near Maleme. The landscape becomes grander, though round (24 m.) *Kakópetros* the hills are clothed in trees. A monument to a patriot hanged by the Germans in 1944 stands at the far end of this village. The terrain becomes rough and mountainous and from c. 1600 ft we get a brief retrospective view of the sea near Kastelli (r.) before passing, at 26 m., through a cut and entering a long enclosed pass. The watershed is not apparent. On the descent the road, widened and realined, affords views of (36¼ m.) *Kándanos* (1892 ft), the chief place of the eparchy of Selino, with a prominent modern church. The town was destroyed by the Germans in 1941; at the entrance (l.) are the waterworks given by a German group as an act of atonement (plaque).

In the outlying villages are three old churches with good frescoes: the Panayia (14C; note especially the scene at the empty Tomb); Ayia Anna (1457–62) at *Anisaráki* (to the N.E.) with scenes from the life of St Anne; and Mikhail Arkhangelos at *Kavalarianá* (to the N.W.), where the frescoes are by Ioannis Pagomenos (1327–28). *Drys*, to the N.W. of Kandanos, also has a frescoed church (1381–91).

We continue to descend in an upland valley growing fruit.—38 m. *Plemenianá* is another village with a frescoed church. We pass high above a rugged gorge and, beyond Kálamos, cross it and run down to the shore.—48 m. **Palaiokhóra** (*Livikon*, modest, **D**; rooms to let), the *Castel Selino* of the Venetians, who built a fort on the promontory in 1279, is now a sizeable village (890 inhab.) straddling the base of the peninsula. There is a large sandy beach, backed by trees. The entrance to the *Frourion* is by the church; the enceinte provides good mountain views to the E., but a better idea of the walls is obtained from the beach below.

Boats may be hired (ask for Kostas Lougiakis) to visit ancient Lissos (c. 1 hr.), Soúia (c. 1¼ hr), etc., and there is a regular caique service twice weekly in summer to Ayía Rouméli and Khóra Sfakíon.

INDEX

Topographical names are printed in **bold** type (modern names) or SMALL CAPS (ancient or medieval names); names of eminent persons in *italics;* other entries in Roman type.

Set by Cold Composition Ltd, Tonbridge, Kent

Printed in Great Britain by Fletcher & Son Ltd, Norwich